THE SECRETS OF PHYSICAL SCIENCE

JOSEPH MIDTHUN   SAMUEL HITI

A CARTOON GUIDE

WORLD BOOK

www.worldbook.com

World Book, Inc.
180 North LaSalle Street
Suite 900
Chicago, Illinois 60601
USA

For information about other World Book publications, visit our website at www.worldbook.com or call 1-800-WORLDBK (967-5325).
For information about sales to schools and libraries, call 1-800-975-3250 (United States), or 1-800-837-5365 (Canada).

The content in this title was previously published as
Building Blocks of Science: Magnetism
Building Blocks of Science: Force and Motion
Building Blocks of Science: Energy
Building Blocks of Science: Gravity
Building Blocks of Science: Matter and How It Changes
Building Blocks of Science: Matter and Its Properties
Building Blocks of Science: Electricity
Building Blocks of Science: Heat
Building Blocks of Science: Sound
Building Blocks of Science: Light

This edition:
The Secrets of Physical Science: A Cartoon Guide
ISBN: 978-0-7166-3632-8 (pbk.)

Printed in the United States of America by
Sheridan Books, Inc.
Chelsea, Michigan

Acknowledgments
Created by Samuel Hiti and Joseph Midthun
Art by Samuel Hiti
Cover by Melanie Bender
Written by Joseph Midthun

TABLE OF CONTENTS

There is a glossary on page 308. Terms defined in the glossary
are in type **that looks like this** on their first appearance in each section.

MAGNETISM

WHAT IS MAGNETISM?

MAGNETIC MATERIALS

Magnets and magnetic materials stick together through thick and thin!

9

TYPES OF MAGNETS

Magnets can have different shapes.

Some magnets are shaped like bars.

These magnets are called bar magnets.

Horseshoe magnets are shaped like the letter "U" or a horseshoe.

Magnets can have other shapes, too.

Magnets can be weak...

...or strong.

MAGNETIC POLES

A magnet has two opposing sides: positive and negative.

They are also called the north pole and the south pole.

For example, a bar magnet has a **pole** on each end.

A horseshoe magnet has a pole on each tip.

N S

N S

If you cut a magnet in half, each separate piece still has two poles.

Whoa.

N S | N S

S N

N S

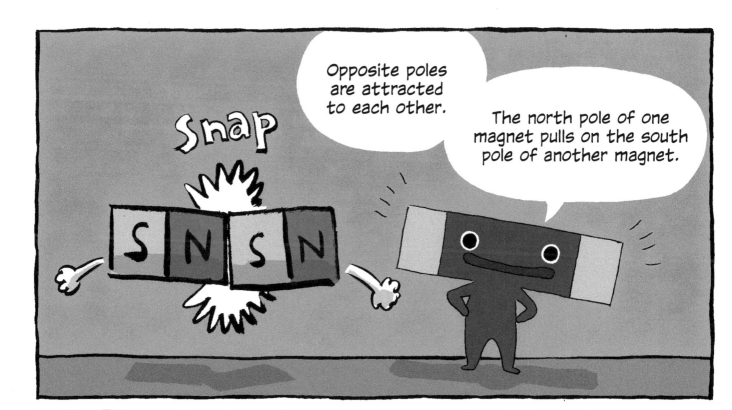

MAGNETIC FIELDS

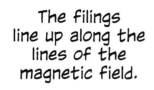

The filings line up along the lines of the magnetic field.

The lines of the field stretch from one pole to the other.

The lines are closer together near the poles.

This shows that the magnetic field is strongest near the poles.

HOW DO MAGNETS WORK?

See for yourself! Try stroking an iron or steel object with a magnet several times in the same direction.

Let's look at what's happening inside.

The poles of the magnetic particles are beginning to line up.

After about 50 strokes, all the poles line up.

They've been magnetized!

After some time, the poles will begin to point in different directions again.

The object no longer acts as a magnet.

TINK   TINK

The inside of Earth is made mostly of melted iron and nickel.

The metals are swirling around inside, creating a magnetic field.

As a result, all of Earth is surrounded by a giant magnetic field.

One pole of the magnet is in the Arctic. The other pole is in Antarctica.

The sun and many planets are magnets, too.

HOW COMPASSES USE MAGNETS

The pole of the compass needle is attracted to the opposite magnetic pole of Earth.

Earth sure is a big magnet!

Did you know that some animals use compasses, too?

Scientists think that some insects, birds, and fish find their way by using tiny natural magnets inside their bodies.

The magnets act like built-in compasses!

ELECTRICITY AND MAGNETISM

An **electromagnet** is a temporary magnet produced by running electric current through a metal object.

A simple electromagnet consists of a coil of wire wrapped around a piece of iron.

ZAP

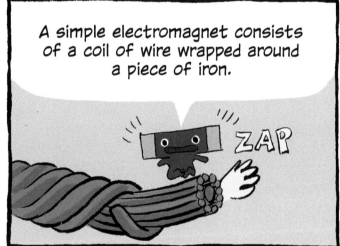

Electricity is then run through the wire.

Electromagnets are useful because they form temporary magnets.

Their magnetic fields can be turned on or off!

Powerful electromagnets are used to lift large objects, like cars at a junkyard.

SHUNK

HOW WE USE ELECTROMAGNETISM

Many machines use electromagnets to work.

Electric generators are machines that create electricity.

They use mechanical energy to create electric energy.

In a generator, magnets and a coil of wire spin around each other.

The spinning produces an **electric current** in the wire.

Power plants use huge generators to produce electricity.

Most generators use steam or water to spin the magnets and wire coil.

Electric motors are used to power such machines as blenders, fans, and vacuum cleaners.

Like generators, electric motors use magnets and coils of wire.

But unlike generators, they use electric energy to create mechanical energy.

In an electric motor, electric current turns on a set of electromagnets, creating a magnetic field.

The magnetic field forces the coil of wire to spin.

VRRRRR

In some parts of the world, you can ride on trains that float above the train tracks!

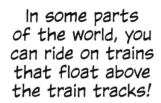

These trains are called maglevs. They use magnetic **repulsion** to move along the tracks.

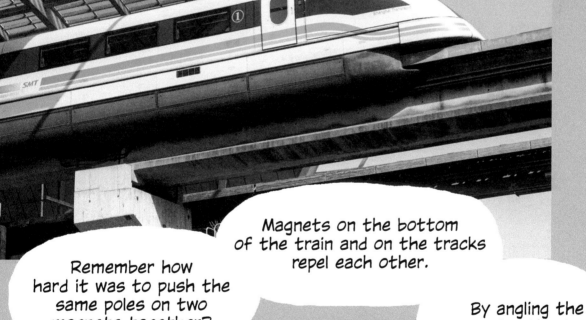

Remember how hard it was to push the same poles on two magnets together?

Magnets on the bottom of the train and on the tracks repel each other.

By angling the magnets, the train can move forward!

WHY STUDY MAGNETISM?

Today, some of the most advanced experiments are made possible by magnets.

The Large Hadron Collider (LHC) is a huge machine that runs in a circle beneath the border of France and Switzerland.

It's like a race track for particles, or more like a demolition derby...

VRROOM

Scientists use the LHC to speed up particles and crash them into one another!

CRASH

Remember: some particles are strongly affected by magnetism, so electromagnets can be used to control the flow of the particles.

The force of magnetism can be used to propel the particles to near the **speed** of light!

By smashing particles together, scientists can recreate the extreme conditions that occurred around the time when the **universe** was formed!

Magnetism could help unlock mysteries of the universe that have evaded humankind for thousands of years!

Particle Particle

SMASH

That's right!

It's up to you, now...

How will you use your new understanding of me?

I'm **MAGNETISM!**

FORCE AND MOTION

WHAT IS A FORCE?

FORCES ALL AROUND US

There are many forces around you every day.

Look at this bulldozer!

That's a mechanical force at work.

That's a lot of force!

Remember gravity?

An astronaut on the moon feels only about a sixth of the gravity you feel on Earth!

Magnetism is another kind of force. Magnets can push or pull!

That can cause motion!

CLANK

ZIP

WHAT IS MOTION?

CHANGING MOTION

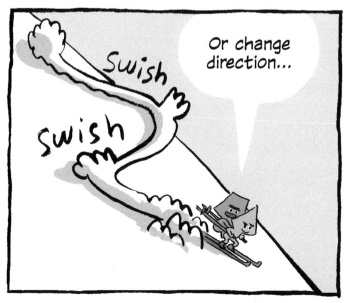

43

Because of inertia, an object in motion tends to keep going at the same speed in the same direction.

The amount of inertia an object has is related to its **mass**—how much **matter** it contains.

The more mass an object has, the more inertia it has.

For example, a heavy object at rest is harder to start moving than a lighter object.

The heavier object has more inertia.

EEK!

PUSH

A heavy object in motion is harder to stop than a lighter object.

STOP!

This boulder sure had a lot of inertia.

That's right!

PEEL

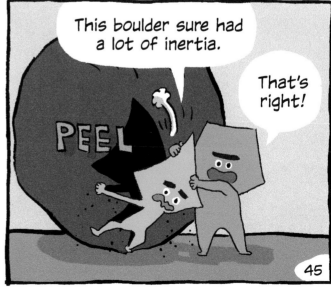

FRICTION

Friction is the rubbing of one object or substance against another.

This rubbing causes resistance between the two surfaces.

When you push on the brakes, the brake pads push against the wheel of your tire. Friction between the pads and the wheel causes your bike to slow down.

But I can slow down when I'm not pressing the brakes, too.

That's because of the friction between the tires and the street.

Friction also makes heat.

That's why you can rub two sticks together to make fire.

RUB RUB RUB

Heat and rubbing can cause objects to wear down!

Oil and other liquids are used on moving machine parts to reduce friction.

Glug Glug Glug

That's why you put oil in your car engine.

Lubrication!

With less friction, parts of the engine move more easily and make less heat.

DOING WORK

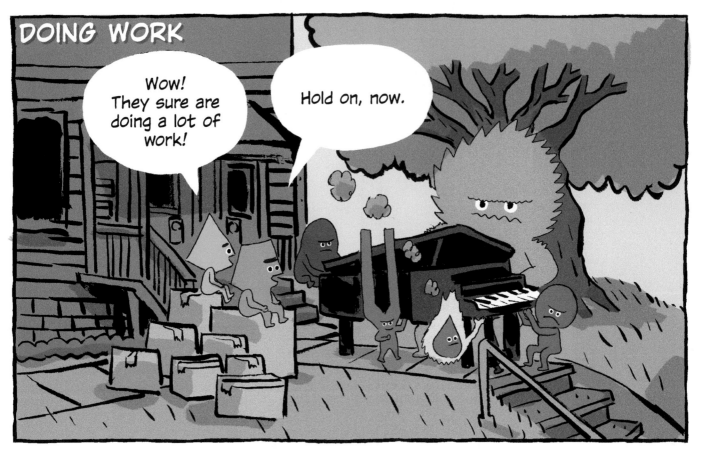

MACHINES AND WORK

But some machines have few or no moving parts.

Simple machines make jobs like moving heavy objects easier.

A machine changes the amount of force you need to use to do work.

It may let you pull in a different direction or allow you to use less force.

The ancient Egyptians built grand pyramids with the help of simple machines. They cut huge limestone blocks with copper chisels and saws.

TINK TINK TINK

They dragged them up long ramps of earth and brick to build each layer of the pyramid.

Done and done.

PLOP

The Egyptians couldn't have made the pyramids without the help of simple machines.

SIMPLE MACHINES

There are six kinds of simple machines.

An **inclined plane** is a flat, slanted surface. It can be used to raise heavy loads.

A **lever** is a bar that moves on a fixed point.

CLANK

Scratch Scratch

A **wheel and axle** is a kind of lever made up of a wheel that moves around a post.

RRRRT!

VROOM!

VROOM!

WHAT IS ENERGY?

How do you move?

Do you walk, run, or jump?

Do you leap over mountains, fly through the sky, or barrel through brick walls?

If you do, you use me!

I'm **ENERGY!**

Energy makes things move and do work.

Cars, trains, and airplanes use energy to take us from place to place.

63

Energy can also cause an object to change form.

You need to use me if you want to bend **metal**.

TWIST

When you burn wood, the heat energy from the fire turns the wood to ash.

If you apply fire to a pot of water, it will eventually boil.

Heat energy causes the boiling water to change from a liquid into a gas.

whistle

Look at all that energy!

WHERE DOES ENERGY COME FROM?

Almost all of the energy on Earth comes from the sun. Think about that for a second.

Light and heat energy from the sun are what make life on Earth possible.

Plants use energy from the sun to make food.

They use this food energy to live and grow.

Many animals eat plants for energy.

You're an animal!

Even animals that eat other animals get their energy from plants.

Without plants to collect this energy, animals would be in serious trouble!

FORMS OF ENERGY

Energy comes in many different forms.

Heat energy can heat our homes, run machines, melt materials, and make electricity. We can make heat energy by building fires and mixing chemicals.

You can feel heat energy on a nice day. That heat is coming from the sun!

Light energy also comes from the sun and objects like lamps or computer screens.

Sound is a form of energy, too. If you read this sentence out loud, you are using sound energy!

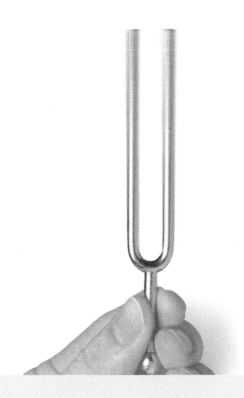

Motion is another form of energy. Just by turning the page, you're using **kinetic energy.**

You may know electric energy as electricity. Electric energy powers nearly all appliances and electronics in your home.

Have you ever seen electricity in nature? That's right! Lightning is a form of electric energy!

ELECTRIC ENERGY

Chemical energy is what makes transportation possible. Most vehicles burn fuel to release its chemical energy.

Chemical energy flows through your body. It comes from the food you eat.

You know what energy looks like when it's in use.

When I jump over these hurdles...

I'm using kinetic energy to move fast!

WOOHOO!

But energy can be stored for later too! This is called **potential energy**.

POTENTIAL ENERGY

Take this wind-up toy.

As I wind it, the spring inside the toy stores the kinetic energy of each turn.

TWIST TWIST TWIST

When the spring is released, its potential energy turns into kinetic energy.

If the spring is released slowly, the dog walks.

YIP YIP YIP

72

But if I wind it too tight...

BOING

Humans use potential energy all the time.

This cell phone is powered by a battery.

Many objects around us are powered by batteries.

Batteries store chemical energy and release it as electric energy.

Potential energy can also be found in nature.

This piece of coal stores chemical energy.

When we burn the coal, its chemical energy turns into heat energy.

Potential energy allows us to store energy to use later.

73

CHANGING ENERGY

Another thing you need to know about energy: it's indestructible!

Energy can't be created or destroyed. It simply moves around and changes form.

Can you think of how your body changes energy? How about when you eat?

Your body changes the chemical energy in food into the kinetic energy that you use whenever you move!

You can see changing energy in nature.

Some deep-sea jellyfish change chemical energy into light energy so that they can glow in the dark!

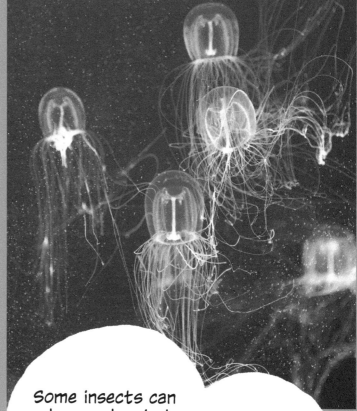

Some insects can change chemical energy into light energy, too. Just look at this firefly...

He is flashing his light to attract mates!

Energy use can be different for every creature!

HOW PEOPLE USE ENERGY

Over time, people have learned how to change one form of energy into another form of energy.

Even prehistoric people knew how to do this.

On cold days, they could burn wood to make a fire.

They probably didn't know it, but they were changing the wood's chemical energy into heat energy!

The ability to change energy into more useful forms is what makes modern life possible.

Today, one of the most useful forms of energy is electric energy.

Look around you. How many things are using electricity?

If there's a computer or TV nearby, you can be sure that they're running on electricity.

And how about your lights?

What about your music player? It uses the stored electricity inside batteries.

Many of the things we do require electricity.

MUSIC

We create this electricity by changing other forms of energy into electric energy.

But it takes an energy source to do so...

FOSSIL FUELS

An energy source is something we can use to make a more useful form of energy.

People use energy sources to make fuel, heat buildings, and to create electricity.

Most of the energy we use comes from burning **fossil fuels.**

Fossil fuels were formed from the remains of living things that died millions of years ago.

Coal, oil, and natural gas are fossil fuels, and they all pack a lot of energy!

Coal is a black or brown rock that can be burned.

Most coal is burned to make electricity.

Natural gas is often burned to heat buildings and cook food.

Oil is made into gasoline for vehicles and fuel oil for homes.

It takes millions of years for fossil fuels to form.

CLunka CLunka

CLunka CLunka CLunka

Once fossil fuels are used up, they can't be replaced.

That's why people call them **nonrenewable resources.**

RENEWABLE RESOURCES

Some energy sources can be used and replaced. They're called **renewable resources**.

Energy from the sun is renewable.

The sun shows up every day!

The sun's energy can be used for heat and to make electric energy.

The sun heats Earth, causing air to move around.

You know this moving air as wind! Wind is a renewable energy source.

Humans use **turbines** to change the energy from wind into electric energy.

Moving water can also be used to make electricity.

Heat from deep inside Earth is also renewable.

Earth has a fiery core that is always hot.

People can use this heat energy to make electric energy or for heating.

GEYSER

THE EFFECTS OF ENERGY USE

As you can see, energy use can also have side effects.

Burning fossil fuels causes **pollution**. Pollution is dirt and waste that harms the environment.

When we burn fossil fuels, they release gases into the air.

These gases trap the sun's heat.

These gases are building up in Earth's **atmosphere.**

Cough, Cough.

Most scientists believe that Earth is becoming warmer because of these gases.

Acid rain is also caused by pollution in the air. It harms forests, rivers, lakes, and streams, along with the wildlife that lives there.

Smog is a form of air pollution that affects many large cities. Some breathing problems and other human illnesses are caused by smog.

REDUCING ENERGY USE

So what can you do to help reduce our impact on Earth?

You can be energy efficient— like me!

Being energy efficient means using energy wisely.

It also means taking steps to reduce your energy use.

How about turning off the lights when you leave the room?

click

Or reusing and recycling items instead of throwing them away?

glass

Plastic

What if your family rode bikes instead of driving a car?

You can also take public transportation.

Reducing your energy use may encourage others to do so, too!

Today, people are working to make renewable energy sources that are as useful as fossil fuels but less harmful.

Every year, scientists create more powerful **solar** panels that collect energy from the sun.

This energy provides a renewable source of electricity.

People have even built airplanes that use solar power!

VRROOM VROOM

Biofuels are fuels made from plants and other natural matter. They can be burned in place of fossil fuels.

Biofuels made from corn are already used in many vehicles.

Scientists are working on fuels made from plants that can grow more easily and quickly than corn.

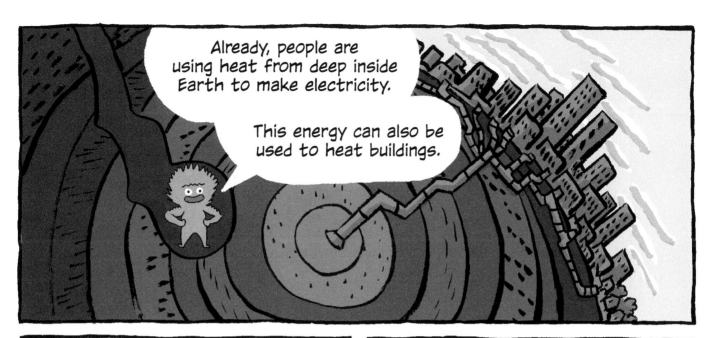

87

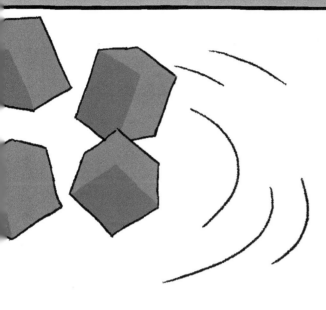

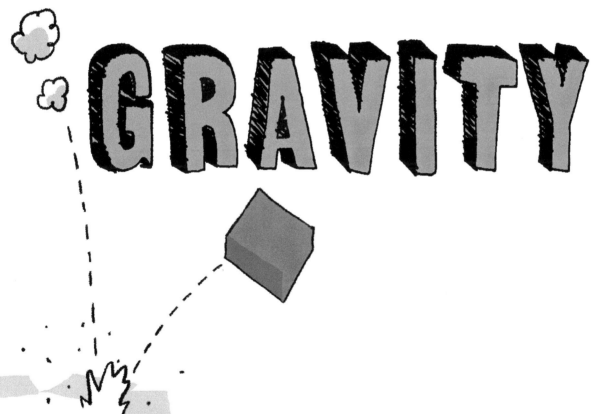

All objects **attract** one another. This **force** is called gravity.

A force is something that pushes or pulls an object.

Gravity is the force that keeps your feet on the ground.

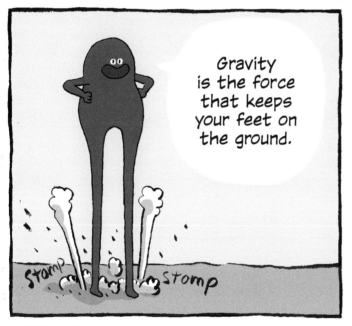

If there were no such thing as gravity...

...you would fly up into the air and off into space.

How can I be so powerful?!

The strength of gravity depends on two things: **distance** and **mass.**

Distance is the space between two objects.

The farther apart two objects are from each other, the weaker the pull of gravity between them.

ZIP

ZIP

Mass measures how much **matter** an object holds.

Everything is made of matter.

Hi.

The more mass an object has, the more it pulls on objects around it.

Gravity!

All objects have gravity— even you!

Your body's gravity pulls Earth toward you.

CLUNK

But Earth has trillions and trillions times more mass than you do.

Earth's gravity pulls you toward the ground.

That's why you can only jump so high!

BOING

MEASURING GRAVITY

Gravity is an invisible force, but we can still measure it.

Weight is a measure of the pull of gravity on an object.

You've probably weighed things to find out how heavy they are. When we weigh things to find out their mass, we use pounds or kilograms as units of measurement.

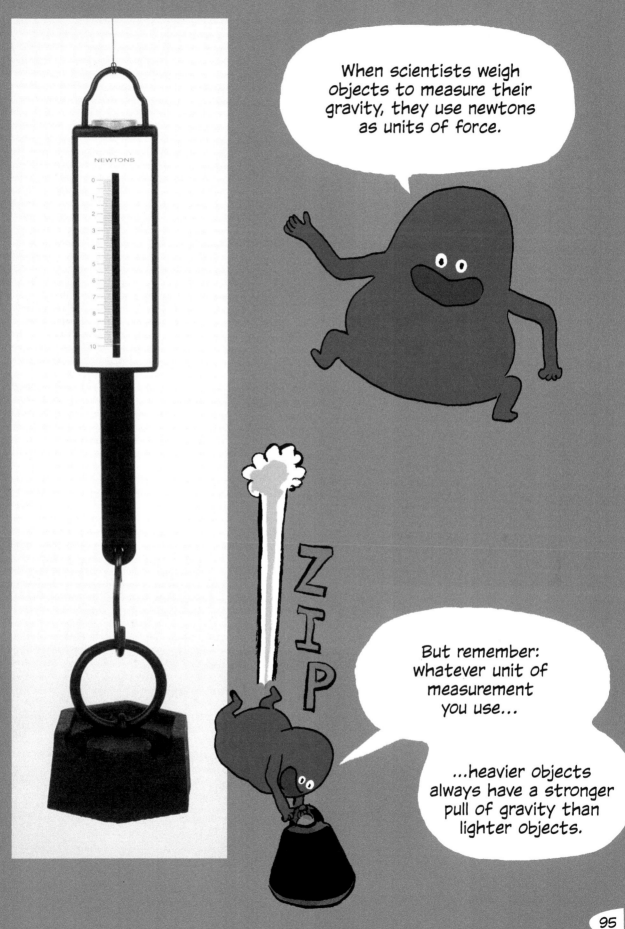

When scientists weigh objects to measure their gravity, they use newtons as units of force.

ZIP

But remember: whatever unit of measurement you use...

...heavier objects always have a stronger pull of gravity than lighter objects.

MASS VS. WEIGHT

In space, your weight would be different than on Earth, even though your mass stays the same.

The moon has less mass than Earth, so its gravity is weaker.

Therefore, you'd weigh less on the moon.

Shunk

G

Jupiter has more mass than Earth, so its gravity is stronger.

You would weigh about 2 1/2 times more on Jupiter than you would on Earth.

HOW OBJECTS FALL

How does gravity affect falling objects? Let's take a look.

If I drop this object from a short distance...

...it's unharmed.

SwiF

CLUNK!

But if I drop it from a great distance...

ZIP

...it breaks.

Crash

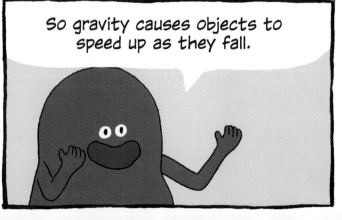

So gravity causes objects to speed up as they fall.

But do all objects fall at the same **speed?**

You may guess that this hammer will fall faster than this feather—

and you're right!

CLUNK

But if gravity affects all matter the same way, all objects should fall at the same speed.

So why does a hammer fall faster than a feather?

Tunk Tunk Tunk Tunk Tunk   Tunk Tunk Tunk Tunk Tunk

Because of **friction!**

FRICTION

FRICTION

Friction makes two objects resist each other when one is pushed or pulled across the other. It causes moving objects to slow down or stop.

SKreeeeh!

ZIP

A falling object experiences friction.

The friction comes from tiny, invisible pieces of matter in the air.

The size, shape, and weight of an object determine how fast or slow it will fall through this matter.

TUNK

As you can see, it is easier for a hammer to pass through the air than a feather.

INERTIA

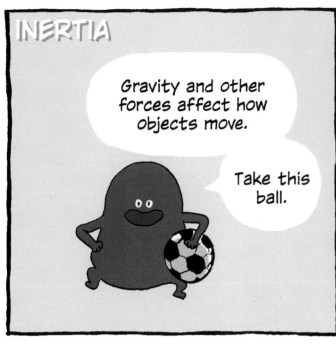

Gravity and other forces affect how objects move.

Take this ball.

If you kick this ball on Earth, it will eventually fall to the ground.

Why?

Because Earth is full of forces that change the ball's **motion**.

kick

TUMP

If you kicked the ball on the moon, it would soar!

kick

SOARRR

On Jupiter it would hardly move at all.

kick

Tump

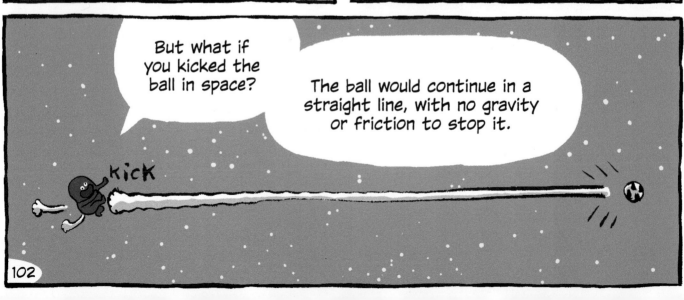

But what if you kicked the ball in space?

The ball would continue in a straight line, with no gravity or friction to stop it.

kick

During the 1600's, the English scientist Isaac Newton defined this idea.

HISTORY

He put it this way...

FLIP
FLIP FLIP

An object in motion tends to stay in motion.

An object at rest tends to stay at rest until a force acts on it.

This idea is called **inertia.**

GRAVITY AND THE SUN

You already know that gravity doesn't just affect things on Earth. The planets, moon, and stars have gravity, too.

The sun's gravity keeps the planets in the **solar system** from hurling off into space.

And inertia is the reason why we don't crash into the sun.

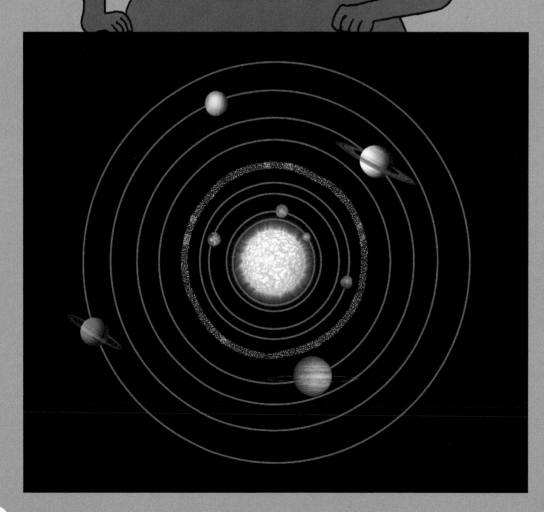

GRAVITY AND THE MOON

We can see the effects of the moon's gravity on Earth's oceans.

Tides are the rising and falling of waters in the oceans and seas. During high tide, a beach might be covered with water.

At low tide, it is uncovered again.

Tides are caused by gravity. They are evidence of the push and pull of gravity between Earth and the moon.

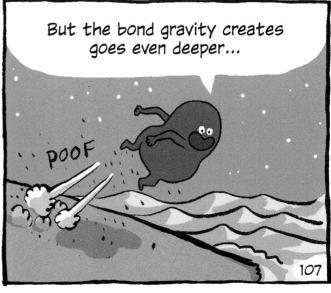

But the bond gravity creates goes even deeper...

POOF

107

GRAVITY AND THE SOLAR SYSTEM

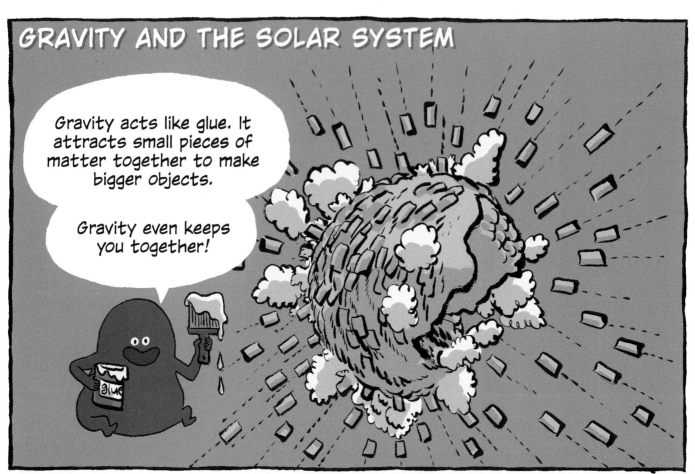

Scientists believe that the entire solar system began as a spinning cloud of gas and dust in space.

As gravity pulled material toward the center, the cloud began to spin faster and faster.

Gravity pulled so much mass together tighter and tighter until a ball of hot gas formed at the center of the cloud.

That ball of fuel still shines today.

Squeaka
Squeaka
Squeaka

We call it the sun.

shif

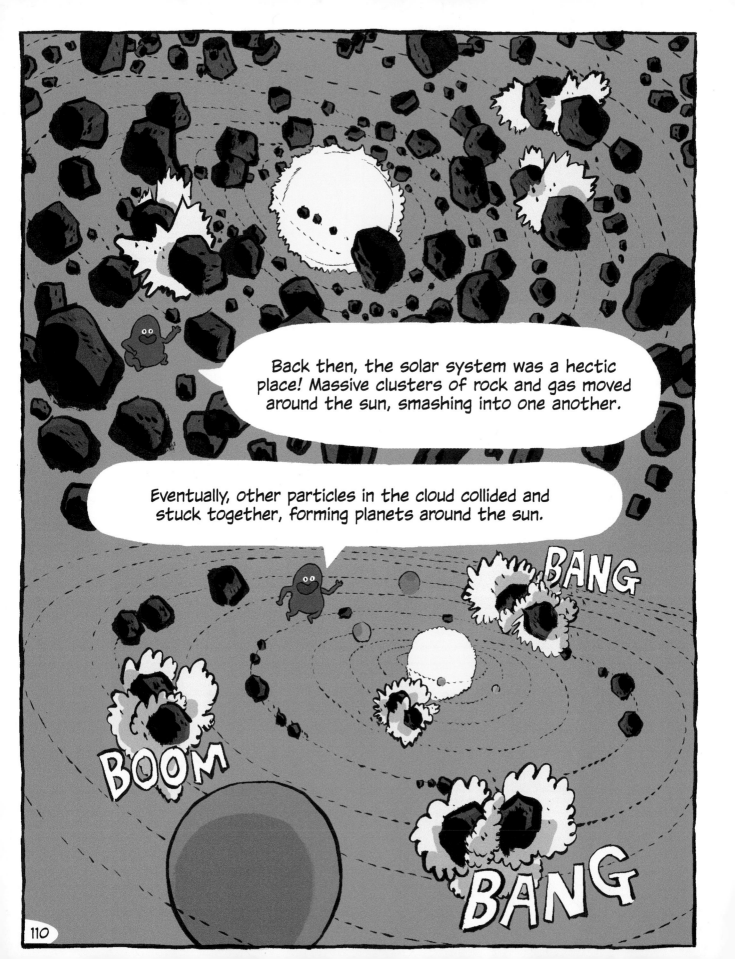

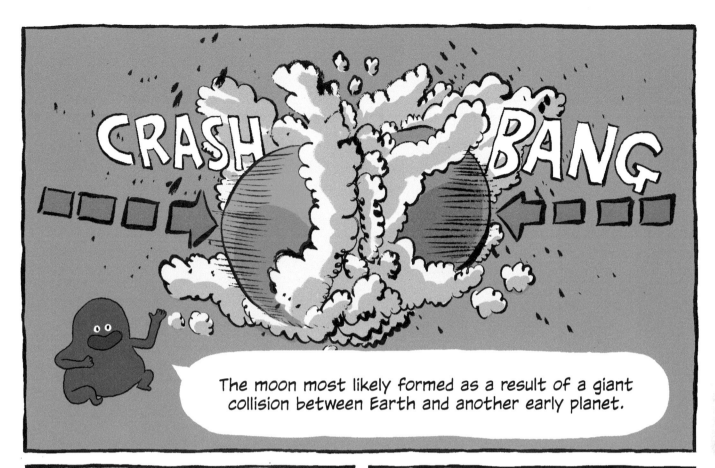

The moon most likely formed as a result of a giant collision between Earth and another early planet.

As a result of the impact, a cloud of rock shot off Earth's surface and went into orbit.

The cloud cooled and **condensed** into a ring of small, solid planetary bodies.

Gravity brought them together, forming the moon!

When a star uses fuel, it releases energy. This energy from inside the star pushes outward.

The star's gravity pulls inward, toward the center of the star.

The star is safe as long as these forces are balanced.

But when the star runs out of fuel, there is nothing to stop the pull of gravity. The star collapses in on itself!

The largest stars keep collapsing until all of their mass collects into one tiny point.

The gravity around a black hole is so powerful it will rip anything apart that comes near.

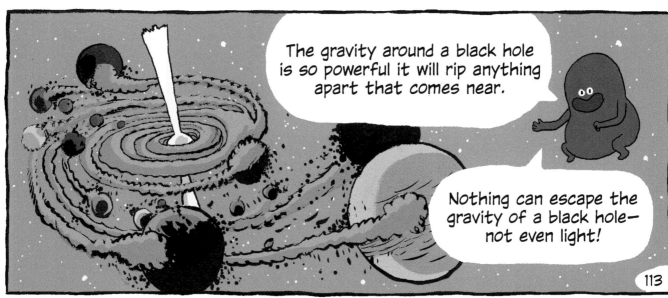

Nothing can escape the gravity of a black hole— not even light!

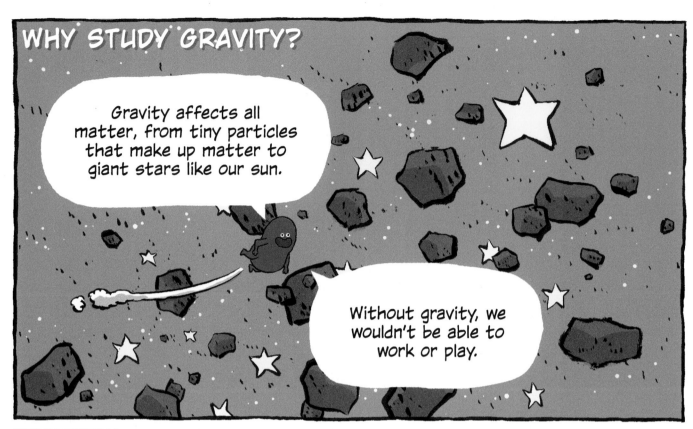

MATTER AND HOW IT CHANGES

CHANGING MATTER

Have you ever wondered how water turns into ice?

When you fill up a tray with water and put it into the freezer...

Hop

Tump

...the water changes from a liquid into a solid.

Atoms are the basic units of matter.

whap

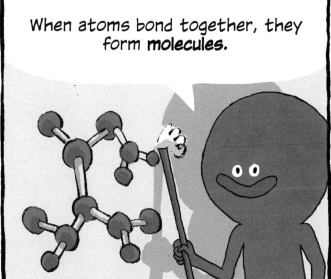

When atoms bond together, they form **molecules.**

LIGHTS, PLEASE!

Let's take a closer look at ice.

It's made of molecules of two hydrogen atoms and one oxygen atom, just like liquid water.

So how come it's frozen solid and not a liquid?

snap

Simple!

Matter can change states, or forms.

STATES OF MATTER

There are three basic **states of matter:** solids, liquids, and gases.

The molecules in a SOLID vibrate. They are arranged in a repeating pattern, like soldiers marching together.

The molecules in a LIQUID move more freely, like people walking in a large group.

The molecules in a GAS are faster. They move even more freely, like people skating in a park.

So what causes matter to change states?

HEATING MATTER

COOLING MATTER

So far, we've changed a solid to a liquid to a gas.

But matter can also change in the reverse direction—from a gas to a liquid to a solid.

Try this.

Make sure your hand is clean and dry.

Now put your hand in front of your mouth and breathe on it.

Your hand will feel damp. Why? The answer is **condensation.**

Your breath contains **water vapor,** a gas. When a gas is cooled, the molecules **condense,** or bundle together.

The gas changes into a liquid.

Your hand is cooler than the inside of your body, so the water vapor changes into liquid water when it hits your hand.

We can see condensation when we breathe on a window. As the water vapor from your breath cools down, tiny droplets of liquid water collect on the glass.

Squeak

127

...AND BACK AND FORTH

Matter can change back and forth between states. This happens around the world every day.

As the sun heats a body of water, the liquid water changes into water vapor.

As water vapor rises into the sky, it begins to cool down. As it cools, the water vapor molecules slow down and pack together into tiny droplets of liquid water.

These tiny droplets make clouds.

The tiny droplets stick together and form larger droplets. These droplets fall back to Earth as rain.

If it is cold enough outside, rain can freeze as it falls, changing from a liquid into a solid—snow!

SCOOP

PHYSICAL CHANGES

A change of state is an example of a **physical change**. The matter may look different, but its **properties** are still the same.

It's still made of the same materials.

If you crumple up or tear a piece of paper, you physically change the paper.

Paper comes from trees.

When I chop down this tree...

chop chop

TIMBER!!!

...it changes from a tree into a log.

CRASH

I can carve this log with a chain saw.

VVVRRR

ZIP

Now all that's left is some sawdust...

BUZ

...and a toothpick!

The tree has just undergone a few physical changes, but it is still wood.

MIXING AND SEPARATING MATTER

We can also cause physical changes by mixing matter together.

Mixtures are physical combinations of substances.

Mixtures can be made of a combination of solids, liquids, or gases.

A sandwich is a simple mixture. Just think, you are combining bread, vegetables, and cheeses together to make lunch!

CHOMP

Some mixtures are more complex, like this ocean water.

The movement of the ocean keeps water and sand evenly mixed.

SCOOP

But if the water is kept still, the larger pieces of sand will settle to the bottom.

This kind of mixture is called a **suspension**.

A suspension is kept mixed by the movement of one or both substances.

When the substances separate, they are no longer a suspension.

133

135

CHEMICAL CHANGES

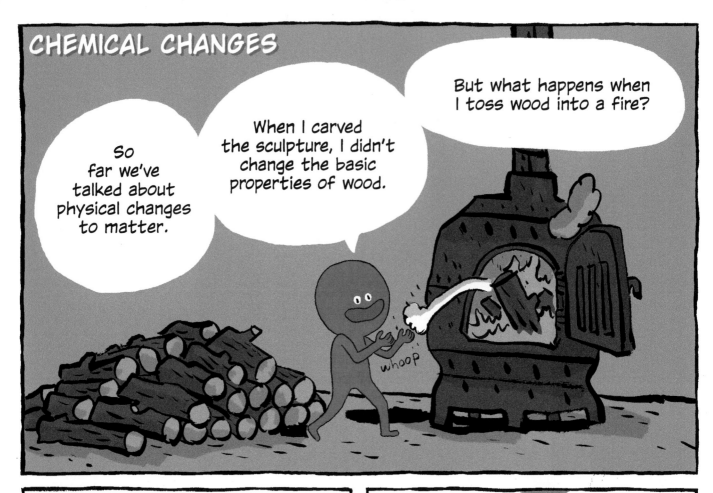

So far we've talked about physical changes to matter.

When I carved the sculpture, I didn't change the basic properties of wood.

But what happens when I toss wood into a fire?

whoop

Fire causes the wood to burn. This is a **chemical change.**

A chemical change causes different kinds of matter to form.

Smoke and ash are made from the carbon, hydrogen, and oxygen atoms that were in the tree.

137

Chemical changes are more common than you might think. Here are some other examples of chemical changes:

When humans eat food, their bodies break down the food into basic **nutrients** that are used for energy.

Green plants use the energy from the sun to combine carbon dioxide and water to make "food" and store it.

Plants use the food energy to live and grow.

PHOTOSYNTHESIS

Humans and other animals can then **absorb** that energy by eating plants or by eating animals that eat plants. They can also release the energy by burning the plant.

COOKING

Food spoils when the tiny living things called **microbes** multiply on the food and begin to eat it.

Microbes produce gases and other chemicals, causing changes in flavor or odor. Rotten food smells bad because of the gases given off by microbes.

YEECCH!

FOOD SPOILAGE

CHANGES AROUND US

Matter changes around us all the time.

Can you think about where you have seen matter change in your day-to-day life?

How about steam coming from radiators...

Or even smoke from a chimney?

tie tie tie

Or what about food?

Have you ever seen someone bake bread? What happens when you put the dough in the oven?

Why do snowplows salt icy roads in the winter?

The salt helps make the ice melt by preventing the water molecules from sticking together. This keeps them from turning into ice.

If we didn't understand the basics of how matter changes...

...we wouldn't be able to do any of these things!

clap
clap
clap

SUPER STATES

Scientists study matter and its different states in laboratories around the world.

They have even discovered some other states of matter!

Super-cold substances create an unusual state of matter.

Superfluids are created by cooling atoms to extremely low temperatures.

ATOMS

A superfluid is a liquid that can behave like a gas.

Liquid   Gas

Helium in a superfluid state can creep up the side of its container and crawl over the lip!

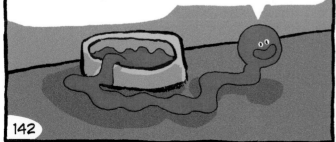

Helium is lighter than air. It is the only **element** that never turns into a solid.

POP

Heating substances to super hot temperatures can change them into an unusual state of matter called plasma.

The sun is made of plasma.

As long as we continue to ask questions and try to understand our world, the possibilities of matter could be endless!

What are *you* going to discover about matter?

MATTER AND ITS PROPERTIES

The ground under your feet is made of matter.

The water in a river is made of matter.

The clouds above you are made of matter.

The stars in the sky are made of matter.

Even *you* are made of matter.

Matter is anything that has **mass** and **volume**.

MASS VOLUME

MEASURING MATTER

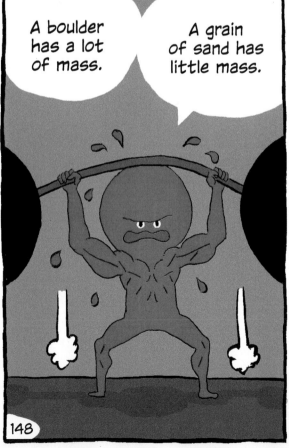

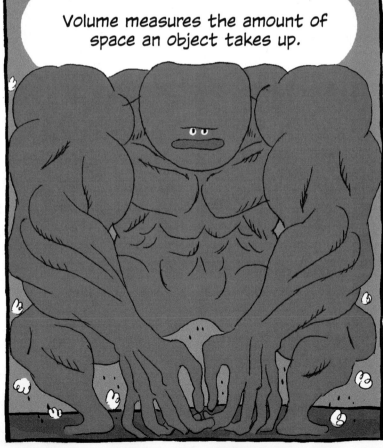

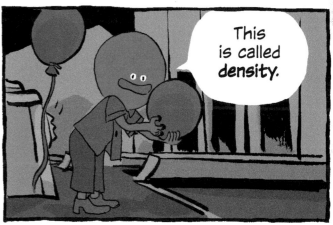

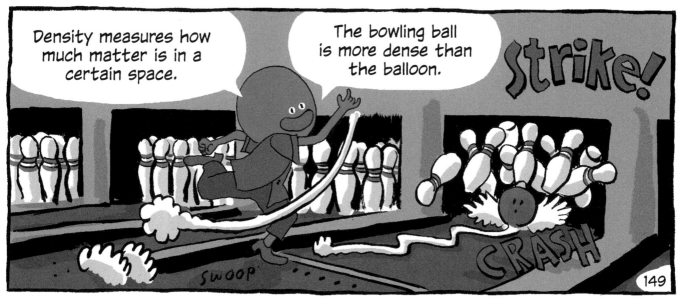

149

PROPERTIES OF MATTER

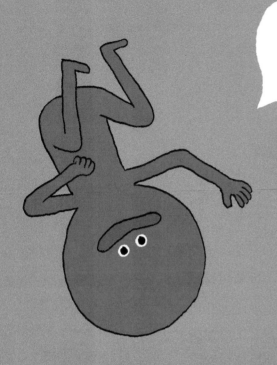

Mass, volume, and density are **properties** of matter.

Properties of matter can be used to describe objects.

COLOR

TEXTURE

SHAPE

SIZE

These pages show examples of some properties of matter you can see or feel.

Some properties of matter are invisible.

But you can test matter to find them.

For example, you can test matter to see...

...whether it floats or sinks.

...if it is **attracted** to magnets.

...if it dissolves in a liquid.

...how easily it melts, freezes, or changes into a gas.

A LOOK INSIDE

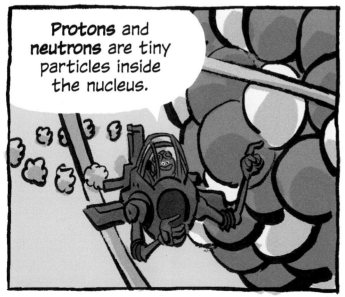

155

ELEMENTS AND COMPOUNDS

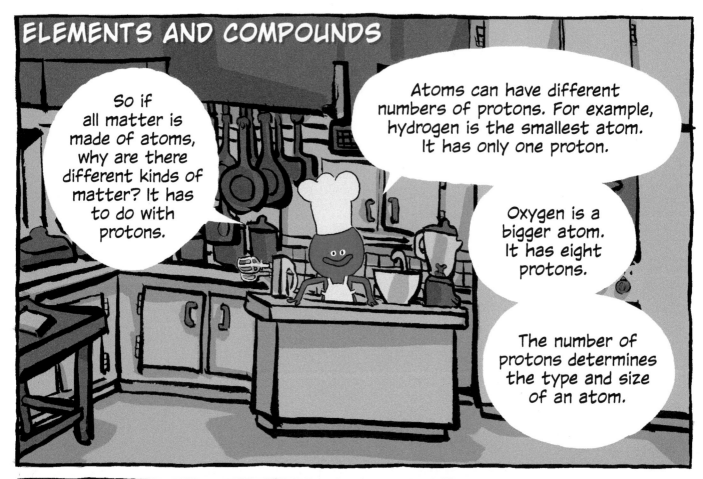

So if all matter is made of atoms, why are there different kinds of matter? It has to do with protons.

Atoms can have different numbers of protons. For example, hydrogen is the smallest atom. It has only one proton.

Oxygen is a bigger atom. It has eight protons.

The number of protons determines the type and size of an atom.

An **element** is another word for a substance with only one type of atom.

Like an ingredient!

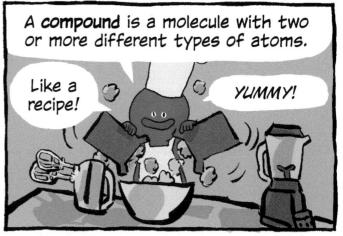

A **compound** is a molecule with two or more different types of atoms.

Like a recipe!

YUMMY!

Let's start with an atom of oxygen.

Oxygen is an element.

Add two atoms of the element hydrogen.

Mix them up and...

STATES OF MATTER

Matter can be a solid, a liquid, or a gas.

In a solid, the molecules move *SLOWLY.*

Solids have a set volume and shape.

In a liquid, the molecules move *FASTER.*

SLURP

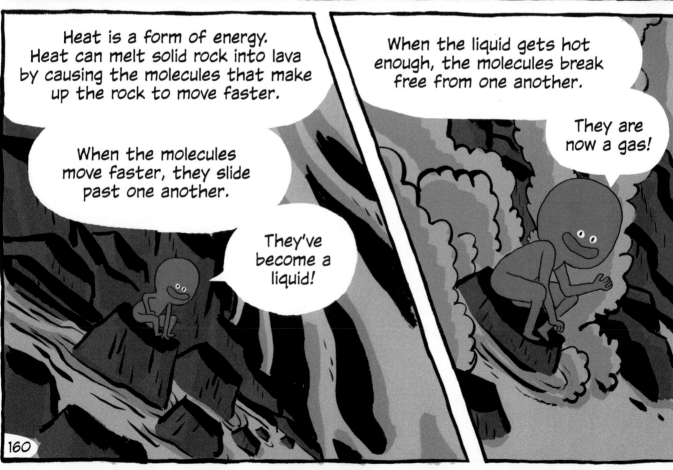

Watch what happens when I toss this giant ice cube into a volcano.

WOOSH

SPLOOSH

The solid ice melts into liquid water...

And the liquid water is changing into...

WATER VAPOR!

A gas!

This can happen in reverse, too.

Water vapor can cool and change into liquid water.

It can cool even more and change into ice, a solid.

161

As you have seen, not all matter is the same.

Scientists group almost all elements of matter into two categories:

Metals and nonmetals.

Metals are a huge group of elements.

They often appear shiny because they **reflect** light well.

Copper, gold, iron, lead, mercury, silver, and tin are examples of metals.

All metals are solids at room temperature *except* mercury, which is a liquid.

The atoms in most metals are closer together than the atoms in nonmetals.

This makes metals more dense.

Metals can be shaped into useful objects.

They can be hammered into thin sheets without breaking.

They can be drawn into wires.

Most metals are also good **conductors** of heat and electricity.

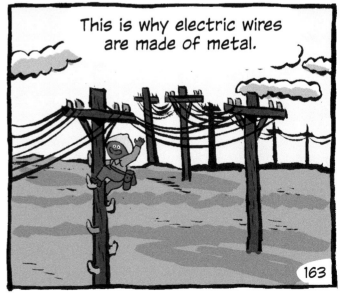

This is why electric wires are made of metal.

THE PERIODIC TABLE

The **periodic table** lists all the elements that scientists have identified so far.

Metals are on one side of the table and nonmetals, except hydrogen, are on the other side.

Each element has its own symbol. Remember when we made a molecule of water?

I called it H_2O.

Here's why!

	1	2	3	4	5	6	7	8	9
1	1 **H** Hydrogen								
2	3 **Li** Lithium	4 **Be** Beryllium							
3	11 **Na** Sodium	12 **Mg** Magnesium							
4	19 **K** Potassium	20 **Ca** Calcium	21 **Sc** Scandium	22 **Ti** Titanium	23 **V** Vanadium	24 **Cr** Chromium	25 **Mn** Manganese	26 **Fe** Iron	27 **Co** Cobalt
5	37 **Rb** Rubidium	38 **Sr** Strontium	39 **Y** Yttrium	40 **Zr** Zirconium	41 **Nb** Niobium	42 **Mo** Molybdenum	43 **Tc** Technetium	44 **Ru** Ruthenium	45 **Rh** Rhodium
6	55 **Cs** Cesium	56 **Ba** Barium		72 **Hf** Hafnium	73 **Ta** Tantalum	74 **W** Tungsten	75 **Re** Rhenium	76 **Os** Osmium	77 **Ir** Iridium
7	87 **Fr** Francium	88 **Ra** Radium		104 **Rf** Rutherfordium	105 **Db** Dubnium	106 **Sg** Seaborgium	107 **Bh** Bohrium	108 **Hs** Hassium	109 **Mt** Meitnerium

57 **La** Lanthanum	58 **Ce** Cerium	59 **Pr** Praseodymium	60 **Nd** Neodymium	61 **Pm** Promethium	62 **Sm** Samarium	63 **Eu** Europium
89 **Ac** Actinium	90 **Th** Thorium	91 **Pa** Protactinium	92 **U** Uranium	93 **Np** Neptunium	94 **Pu** Plutonium	95 **Am** Americium

You can read the table like this...

Atomic Number
Atomic Symbol
Atomic Name

1 **H** Hydrogen

The symbol for hydrogen is *H* — get it?

"H" for hydrogen.

"O" for oxygen.

So the symbol for a molecule of water, two hydrogen atoms and one oxygen atom, is H_2O!

			13	14	15	16	17	18
								2 **He** Helium
			5 **B** Boron	6 **C** Carbon	7 **N** Nitrogen	8 **O** Oxygen	9 **F** Fluorine	10 **Ne** Neon
10	11	12	13 **Al** Aluminum	14 **Si** Silicon	15 **P** Phosphorus	16 **S** Sulfur	17 **Cl** Chlorine	18 **Ar** Argon
28 **Ni** Nickel	29 **Cu** Copper	30 **Zn** Zinc	31 **Ga** Gallium	32 **Ge** Germanium	33 **As** Arsenic	34 **Se** Selenium	35 **Br** Bromine	36 **Kr** Krypton
46 **Pd** Palladium	47 **Ag** Silver	48 **Cd** Cadmium	49 **In** Indium	50 **Sn** Tin	51 **Sb** Antimony	52 **Te** Tellurium	53 **I** Iodine	54 **Xe** Xenon
78 **Pt** Platinum	79 **Au** Gold	80 **Hg** Mercury	81 **Tl** Thallium	82 **Pb** Lead	83 **Bi** Bismuth	84 **Po** Polonium	85 **At** Astatine	86 **Rn** Radon
110 **Ds** Darmstadtium	111 **Rg** Roentgenium	112 **Cn** Copernicium	113 * Unutrium	114 **Fl** Flerovium	115 * Ununpentium	116 **Lv** Livermorium	117 * Ununseptium	118 * Ununoctium

*Atomic symbol to be determined

64 **Gd** Gadolinium	65 **Tb** Terbium	66 **Dy** Dysprosium	67 **Ho** Holmium	68 **Er** Erbium	69 **Tm** Thulium	70 **Yb** Ytterbium	71 **Lu** Lutetium
96 **Cm** Curium	97 **Bk** Berkelium	98 **Cf** Californium	99 **Es** Einsteinium	100 **Fm** Fermium	101 **Md** Mendelevium	102 **No** Nobelium	103 **Lr** Lawrencium

Metals   Metalloids   Nonmetals

MATTER AT WORK

Scientists must understand the properties of matter to make many of the objects you use at home.

Look at this teapot.

It's made to contain water over a fire until it boils.

To make a teapot, you would need to construct it out of an element that would not melt *before* the water boils.

glug glug glug

Scientists need to know the melting point of the elements used to make the teapot.

RIP RIP

169

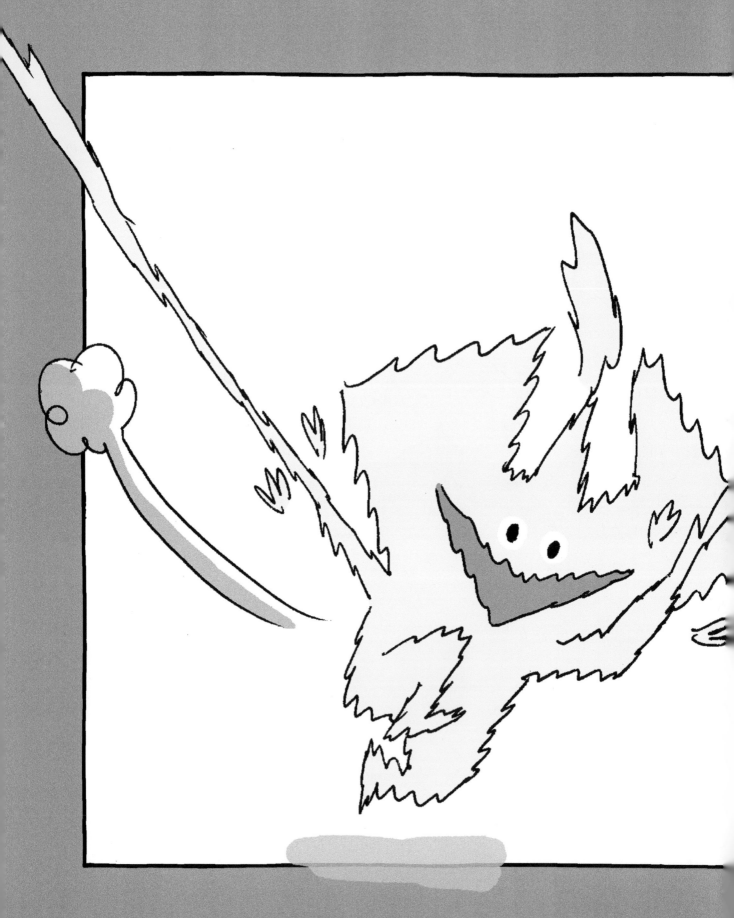

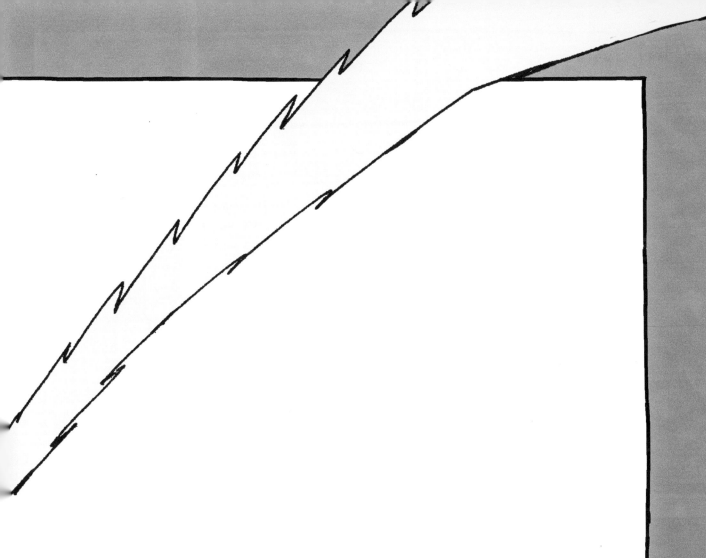

ELECTRICITY

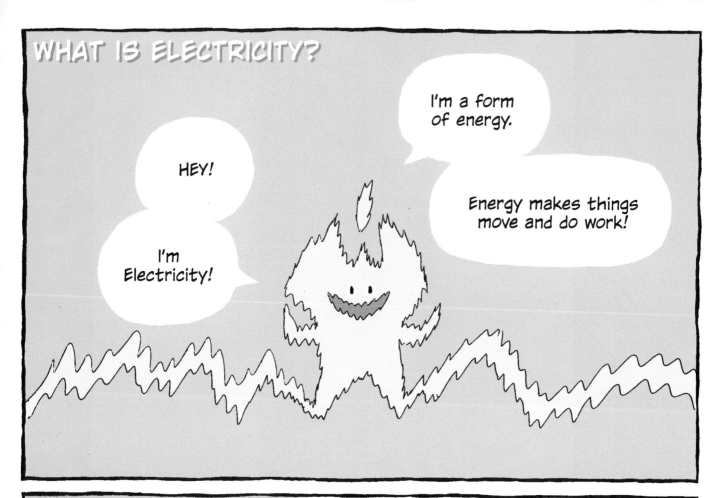

175

I'm inside you right now.

Every action and every thought are a result of electricity.

Electrical signals inside your body carry information to and from your brain.

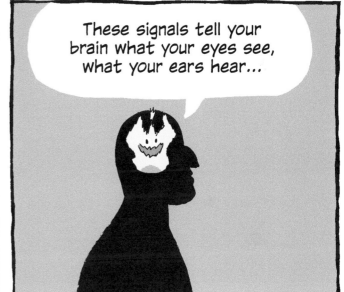

These signals tell your brain what your eyes see, what your ears hear...

...and what your fingers feel.

The signals even tell your heart when to beat!

PUM PUM

PUM PUM

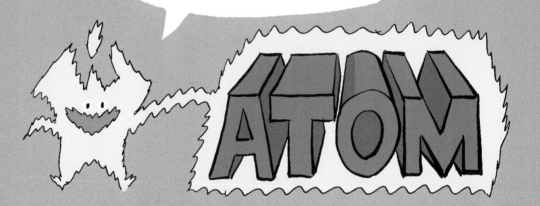

All matter is made of tiny particles called **atoms.**

Atoms are made of even tinier particles.

Particles that carry a positive charge or neutral charge make up the center of an atom.

Electrons are negatively charged particles that circle around the center of an atom.

When atoms have an equal number of positive and negative particles, they have no **electric charge.**

BOO-HOO!

But atoms can gain or lose electrons.

When this happens, an atom becomes electrically charged!

The movement of electrons is what we call electricity.

STATIC ELECTRICITY

The build-up of electrons creates **static electricity.** You've probably experienced static electricity firsthand.

Have you ever shuffled your feet across a carpet and then touched a doorknob?

Rub Rub Rub

What happened?

You probably got an electric shock!

ZAP

The rubbing between your feet and the rug causes electrons to jump from the rug to your body.

This gives your body extra electrons.

You get a negative charge!

When you touch the doorknob, electrons jump from your body to the object.

You feel this movement of electrons as an electric shock.

Electrons tend to move away from areas with a negative charge.

That's why they jumped from your body to the doorknob!

CURRENT ELECTRICITY

People can't use static electricity to power ordinary machines.

That's because the electric charge is released all at once.

PO OM

To make electricity more useful, we must create an **electric current.**

ELECTRIC CURRENT

An electric current is the steady flow of electrons from atom to atom.

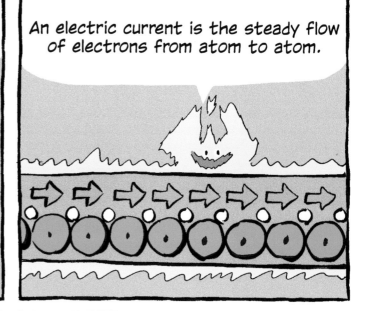

Electric current that we use for energy flows in a loop called a **circuit.**

Think of a circuit as a raceway.

The cars are electrons that race around the track.

VROOM

Simple circuits have three main parts: an energy source, an object that needs electric current to work, and a wire that connects them.

This robot uses batteries as an energy source.

Energy is stored inside the battery's chemicals.

This energy pushes electrons through the circuit.

As the electrons flow, the robot moves!

CIRCUITS AND SWITCHES

In order for this light bulb to work, the circuit must be closed.

That is, it must form a complete loop.

Otherwise, the electric current can't get through.

LOOP

But what if you want to turn the light off?

You can use a **switch**!

Switches allow you to control the flow of current by opening and closing the circuit.

open

Switch

Flip the switch to "on," and the contacts are connected!

Closed

Switch

The circuit is closed. The light is on!

CONDUCTORS AND INSULATORS

Some materials allow electrons to flow more easily.

They're called **conductors**.

Many **metals** are good conductors.

That's why many electrical wires are made of copper or other metals.

Other materials stop the flow of electrons from atom to atom.

These materials are called **insulators**.

Wood, plastic, and rubber are good insulators.

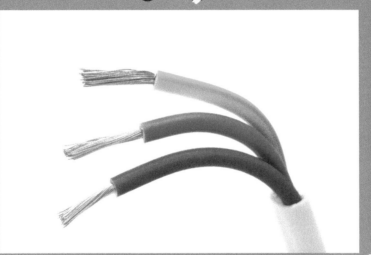

Electrical wires are often covered by rubber or plastic.

These materials keep the electric current in the wire and prevent you from getting an electric shock!

HOW DO WE USE ELECTRICITY?

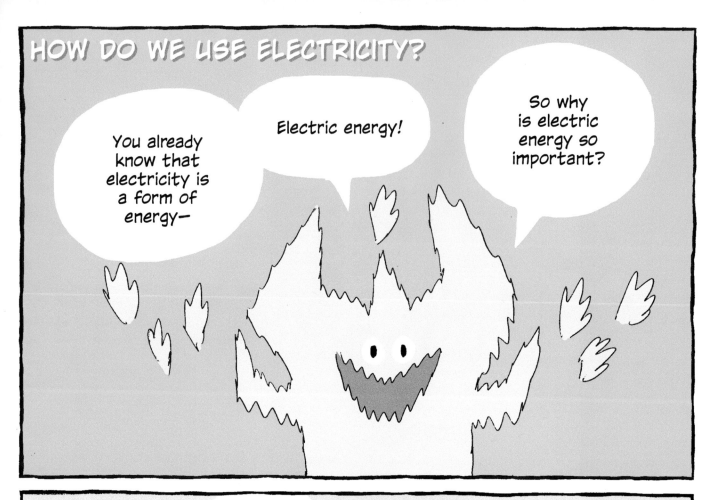

You already know that electricity is a form of energy—

Electric energy!

So why is electric energy so important?

Because we can use it to make many other forms of energy.

Look at the lights around you.

They're using electric energy to make light energy!

Many people use electric energy to heat their homes or cook food.

And machines that use **electric motors** convert electric energy into mechanical energy—

The energy of **motion!**

These things are possible because of me!

GENERATING ELECTRICITY

People use lots of electricity every day.

So where, you might ask, does all this electricity come from?

Power plants!

Power plants use **electric generators** to convert mechanical energy into electric energy.

These giant machines are driven by a **turbine.**

The pressure of steam or falling water spins the blades of the turbine.

The spinning blades cause magnets inside the generator to spin around a metal wire.

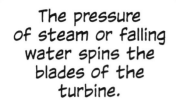

The spinning magnets push and pull on the electrons inside the wire.

The moving electrons create an electric current.

Power plants generate enough current to power entire cities!

Once an electric current is generated, it is directed into the electrical grid.

The electrical grid is a huge circuit.

It is made of power lines and connections that bring electricity to your home.

Your home is connected to the grid by copper wires wrapped in plastic.

These wires run through the walls of your home.

People tap into the grid by plugging a cord into an outlet on the wall.

Presto! The circuit is complete!

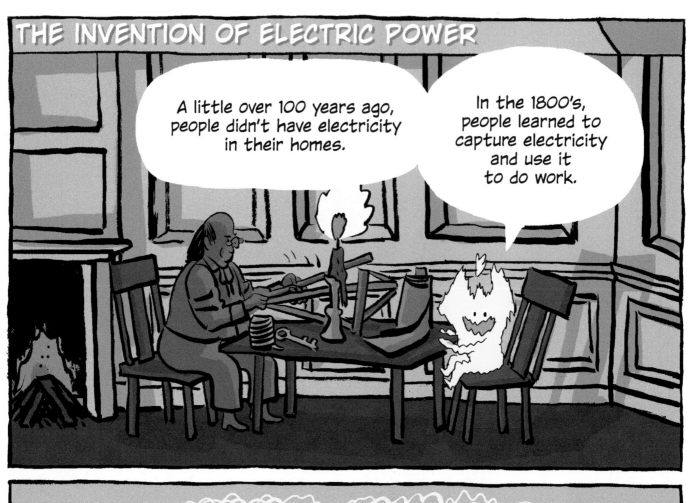

This led to the invention of electric devices, or electronics.

Some devices allowed people to talk across great **distances.**

Others helped people handle information quickly.

Over time, the demand for electricity grew.

Today, most people cannot imagine life without electric power.

But there are negative effects to all this energy use...

SOURCES OF ELECTRIC POWER

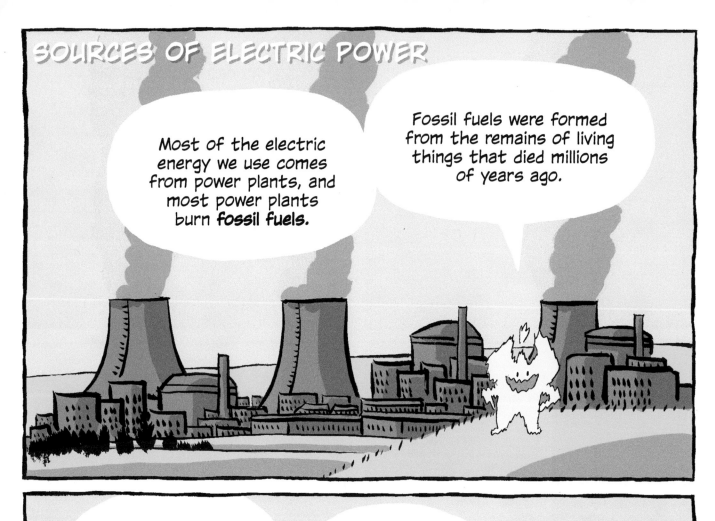

Most of the electric energy we use comes from power plants, and most power plants burn **fossil fuels.**

Fossil fuels were formed from the remains of living things that died millions of years ago.

Many people are worried that Earth's supply of these fuels will be used up.

On top of that, burning these fossil fuels harms our planet.

Scientists have learned how to convert energy from other sources as well.

For instance, this dam uses the power of running water to generate electricity.

And when wind turns the blades of a windmill, a turbine creates electricity!

Some **solar** panels convert the sun's energy into electricity.

Soak up those rays!

REDUCING ELECTRICITY USE

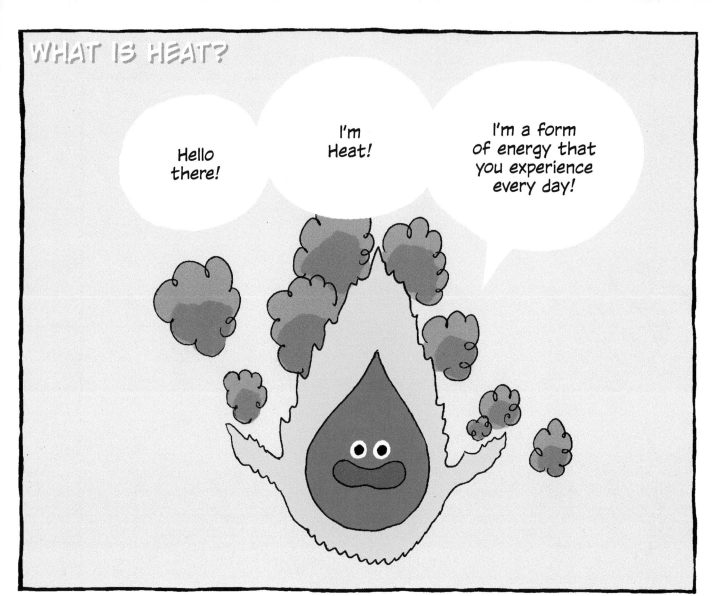

HOW DO WE USE HEAT?

I'm an important part of your life. In fact, I'm inside your body right now.

Your body creates heat when it uses food.

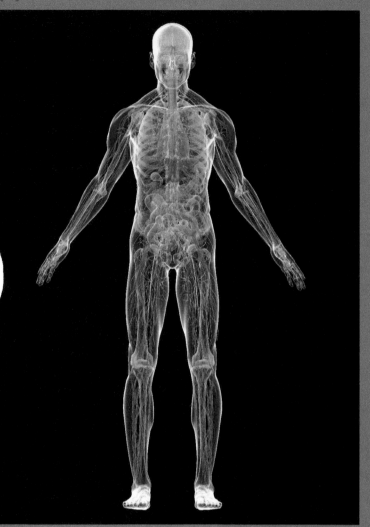

That's how you maintain a steady temperature.

People use heat to cook food and warm their homes.

In factories, heat is used to bend and shape **metals!**

Iron melts at about 3000 degrees Fahrenheit (1535 degrees Celsius)!

Volcanoes, hot springs, and geysers all release heat from inside the planet.

Fires and electricity are other sources of heat.

You can also create heat by rubbing two objects together.

THE FLOW OF HEAT

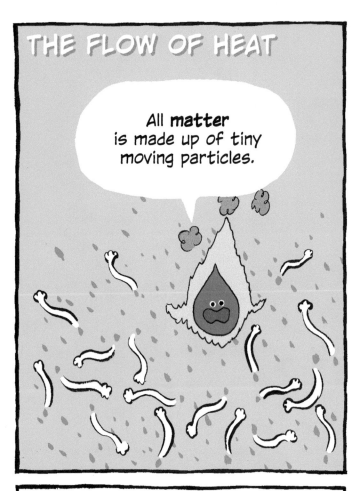

All **matter** is made up of tiny moving particles.

The energy that makes them move is called **thermal energy**.

THERMAL ENERGY

When we heat matter, the thermal energy in its particles increases.

WOOF!

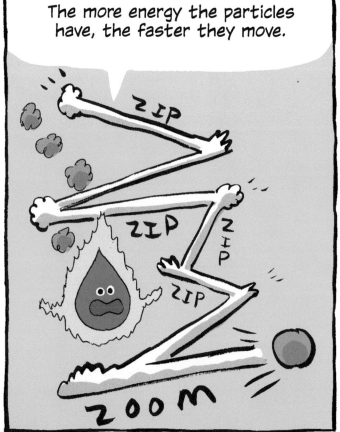

The more energy the particles have, the faster they move.

ZIP

ZIP

ZIP

ZIP

ZOOM

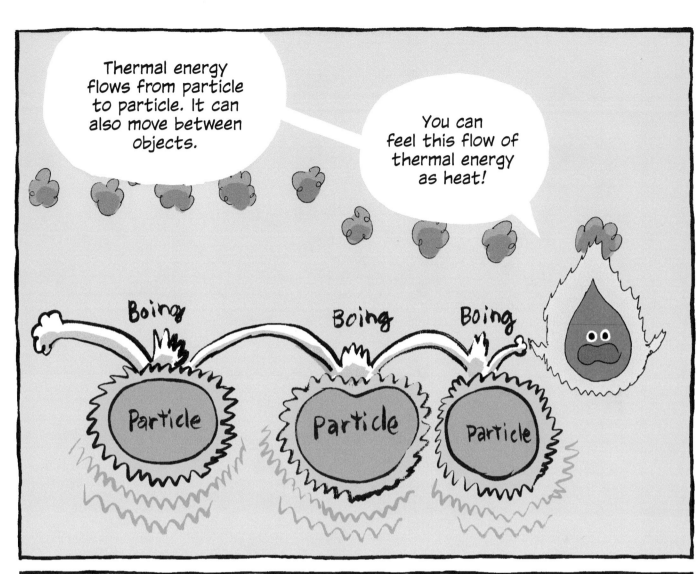

The particles in the ice are moving slowly.

The liquid water is warmer than the ice, so its particles are moving a little faster.

The thermal energy from the liquid water flows to the ice.

Then the particles in the ice speed up.

This causes the ice to melt.

It changes from a solid to a liquid.

Eventually, all the water in the glass becomes the same temperature.

Now, all of the water particles in the glass are moving at the same **speed!**

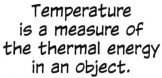
Temperature is a measure of the thermal energy in an object.

Glass **thermometers** use expansion and contraction to measure temperature.

A glass thermometer is filled with a liquid.

When you measure the temperature of something hot, the liquid inside the tube gets heated. It expands and rises.

Keesh

When you measure the temperature of something cold, the liquid contracts. It moves down the tube.

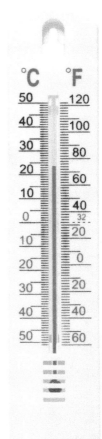

People use thermometers to measure temperature every day. How do you know what kind of clothes to wear?

You measure the temperature outside!

Heating matter can cause it to change physically.

The matter may look different, but it's still made of the same materials.

Take this ice sculpture...

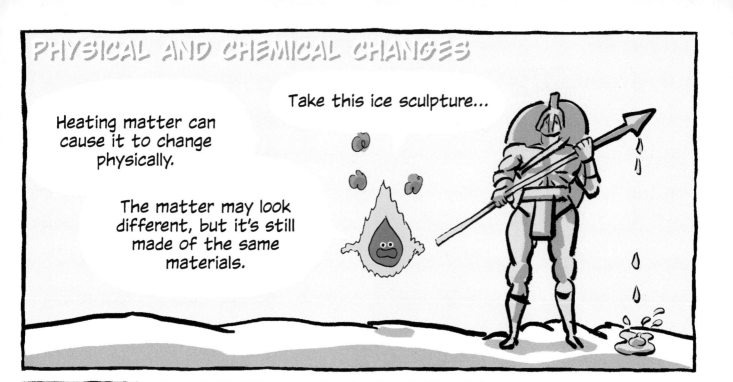

When heat is applied to ice, it melts. It becomes liquid water.

PiP PiP PiP

And when the liquid water is heated, it changes into **water vapor,** a gas. It is still water, just in a different state.

Metals also melt if they are heated to high temperatures.

Sag

This is how we can shape and mold metals into objects.

Heat can also cause some kinds of materials to burn.

Burning is a sign of a **chemical change.**

The substances that make up the matter change into new substances.

This is a **physical change.**

crumple crumple crumple

This is a chemical change.

As you can see, the paper isn't paper anymore. It has changed into something else.

Ash!

Whenever you produce a new substance, that's evidence of a chemical change.

WOOF

CONDUCTION

Heat is always on the move, but I don't always move the same way.

Sometimes I move from particle to particle, much like dominoes tipping over. This allows me to travel through a material.

TIP

The movement of heat from one particle to another is called **conduction.**

CONDUCTION

Solids are often heated by conduction. The particles in solids don't move around freely.

Thermal energy causes them to vibrate in place and bump into nearby particles.

If you leave a metal spoon in a hot pot of food, BEWARE!

The entire spoon will heat up!

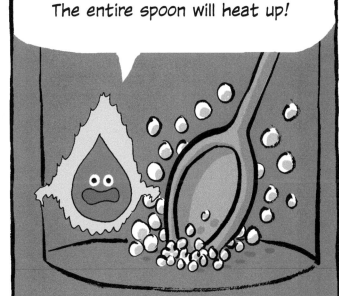

The hot food heats up the tip of the spoon...

Then hot particles in the tip of the spoon shake faster and bump into the particles next to them. This transfers thermal energy.

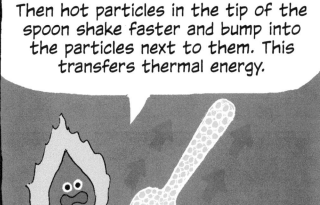

These particles then bump into other particles.

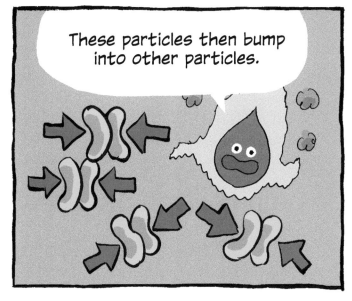

This is how heat moves up the spoon's handle.

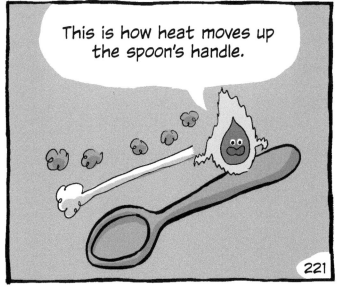

221

CONVECTION AND RADIATION

Heat also uses particles to travel through liquids and gases.

But unlike solids, the particles of liquids and gases can move around more freely.

They can carry heat around with them as they move about.

In a pot of boiling water, heated water at the bottom of the pot expands.

It rises to the top, forcing the cooler water to the bottom. Then the cooler water becomes warm and rises.

This movement of heat is called **convection**. Convection acts like a conveyor belt to move heat from one place to another.

CONVECTION

Some kinds of heat can travel through empty space.

The movement of heat without any matter to carry it is called **radiation.**

RADIATION

Heat from the sun travels through space to warm Earth.

Heat can also be transferred by radiation where matter is present.

Sup?

You can feel the warmth of a nearby fire even if the air is still. Heat from the fire can travel to your skin by radiation.

CONDUCTORS AND INSULATORS

Some materials help heat to move easily between objects.

They're called **conductors.**

Metals are good conductors. I can travel through this pan very easily!

Insulators are materials that reduce the **motion** of heat.

You need an insulator to touch a hot pan.

This oven mitt works great!

A winter jacket is another good insulator.

Winter jackets are made of materials like cotton, nylon, and down feathers.

These materials are insulators.

POOF

They do not conduct much heat away from your body.

Some jackets keep wind from stealing heat away from your body.

Wind carries heat away by convection.

WOOSH

Your home is like a big winter jacket.

Its walls are packed with insulation to keep heat in on cold days and out on hot days.

WHY STUDY HEAT?

Buildings and other structures would crumble to the ground if they were made with no account for different temperatures.

If your jacket were made of a conductor instead of an insulator, you'd freeze!

BRRR!

BRRR!

226

WHAT MAKES SOUND?

When an object vibrates...

...the air around the object vibrates, too!

These vibrations in the air are called **sound waves.**

HOW DO WE HEAR SOUNDS?

What happens once a sound reaches your ears?

Let's take a look inside!

ZIP

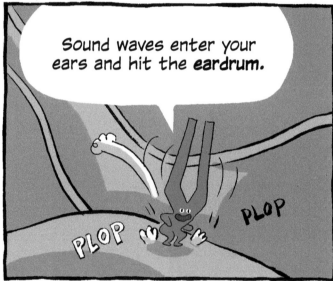

Sound waves enter your ears and hit the **eardrum.**

PLOP   PLOP

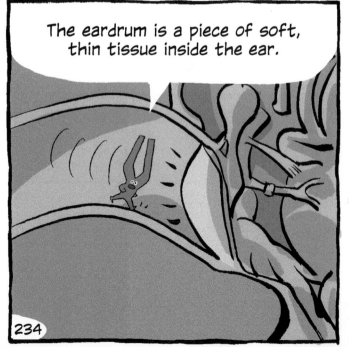

The eardrum is a piece of soft, thin tissue inside the ear.

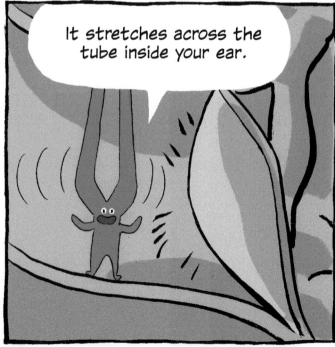

It stretches across the tube inside your ear.

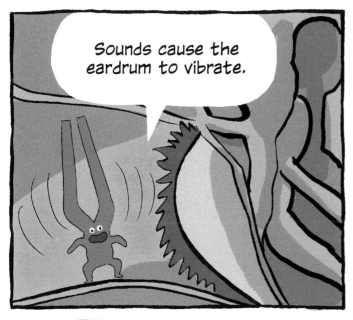

Sounds cause the eardrum to vibrate.

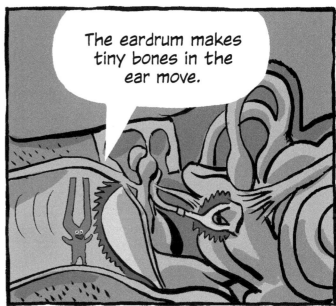

The eardrum makes tiny bones in the ear move.

These bones send the sound to a curled tube deep inside the ear called the **cochlea.**

The cochlea is full of liquid. As the sound waves travel through this liquid, they make tiny hairs bend.

The bending hairs cause nerves to send signals to the brain.

Auditory cortex

Your brain uses these signals to perceive sound.

CARRYING SOUND

Sound can move through any **state of matter**—gas, solid, or liquid.

But I travel faster through solids and liquids than I do through air.

That's because the particles in solids and liquids are closer together than the particles in air.

Listen!

You can probably hear a sound coming from somewhere right now...

ABSORBING SOUND

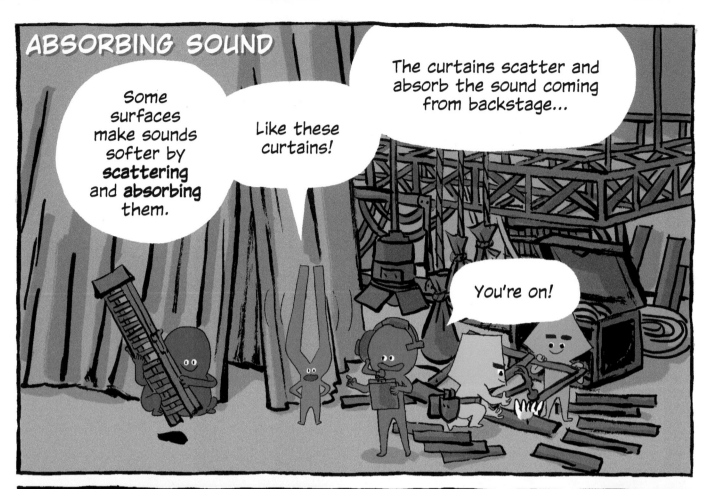

Some surfaces make sounds softer by **scattering** and **absorbing** them.

Like these curtains!

The curtains scatter and absorb the sound coming from backstage...

You're on!

So the audience can listen to the performance and not the stagehands!

Some places need more sound absorption than others.

Recording studios, opera houses, and dance clubs are all built with sound control in mind.

In this concert hall, the seats are cushioned to absorb sound.

Even if the seat is empty, it absorbs as much sound as if someone were there.

This way, a performance will sound the same if there are only a few people or a full house!

BRAVO!

CLAP CLAP CLAP

CLAP CLAP CLAP CLAP

WHAT MAKES AN ECHO?

Some surfaces **reflect** sound. When sounds reflect back at us, we may hear an **echo.**

For example, when you shout, the sound of your voice travels through the air in all directions.

You hear the shout when the sound first reaches your ears.

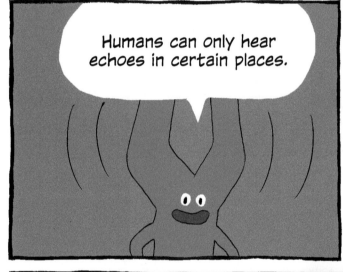

Humans can only hear echoes in certain places.

Like this cave!

LIKE THIS CAVE!

When the sound hits the walls of the cave, it bounces back to your ears a second time.

BOUNCE

Animals with better hearing than humans hear echoes all the time!

Some animals use echoes to navigate and hunt. Bats, dolphins, and whales all use **echolocation.**

A bat can "see" in the dark with sound.

SWOOP

Look out!

Bats make a high-pitched sound and listen to the echoes that are reflected back.

Then the bat can measure the **distance** to a cave wall or even a tasty snack.

Dolphins and whales use echolocation to sense objects and other sea creatures.

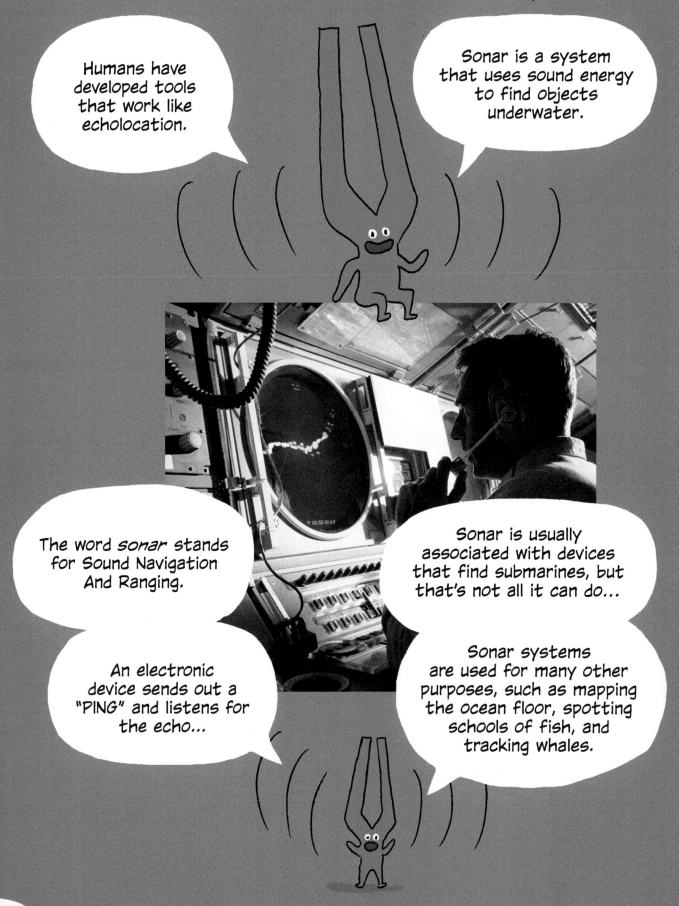

Humans have developed tools that work like echolocation.

Sonar is a system that uses sound energy to find objects underwater.

The word *sonar* stands for Sound Navigation And Ranging.

Sonar is usually associated with devices that find submarines, but that's not all it can do...

An electronic device sends out a "PING" and listens for the echo...

Sonar systems are used for many other purposes, such as mapping the ocean floor, spotting schools of fish, and tracking whales.

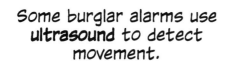
Some burglar alarms use **ultrasound** to detect movement.

Ultrasound is a type of sonar that operates at a frequency above human hearing.

Doctors can use an ultrasound machine to take a peek inside your body!

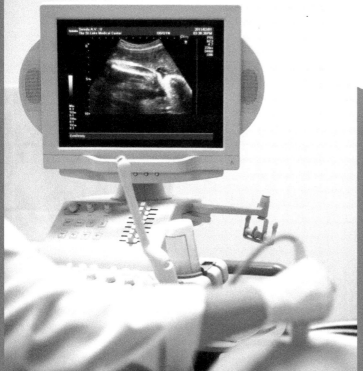

SOUND WAVES

The shape of a sound wave can tell us about the quality of the sound.

Sound waves are somewhat like ocean waves.

They have high points and low points.

The high point of a sound wave is called a **crest,** or peak.

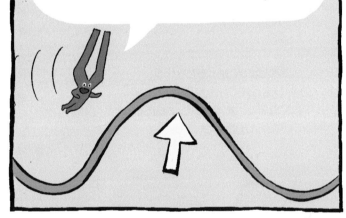

The crest represents the area of crowded particles in a sound wave.

The low point of the sound wave is called a **trough,** or valley.

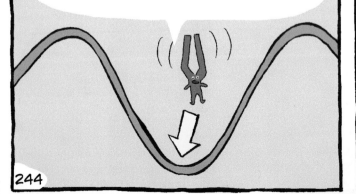

The trough represents the area in a sound wave where the particles are farthest apart.

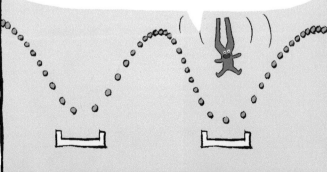

Sound waves are even more similar to the coils in a toy spring.

Watch what happens as this toy spring moves down the stairs.

The coils push together and spread apart.

The coils of the spring that are bunched together are the crests of the wave.

The coils that are spread apart are the troughs!

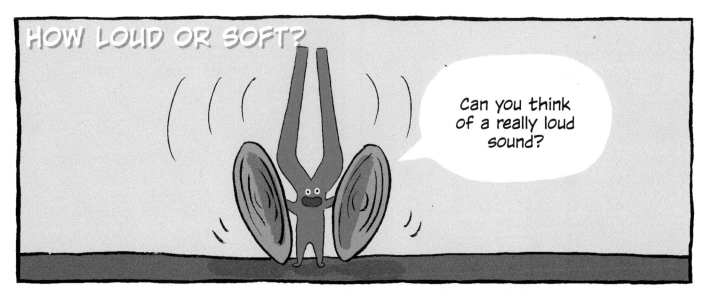

The greater the amplitude...

...the more energy in the wave...

AMPLITUDE

THE LOUDER THE SOUND!

Some sounds you can barely hear at all...

Like a pin drop!

ping

Soft sounds have less energy than loud sounds.

Sounds can be high...

And sounds can be low.

Have you ever wondered what makes a sound high or low?

It has to do with **frequency**.

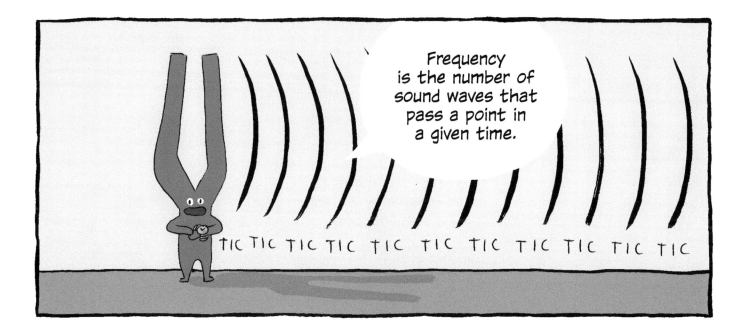

Frequency is the number of sound waves that pass a point in a given time.

TIC TIC TIC TIC TIC TIC TIC TIC TIC TIC TIC

The faster an object vibrates, the greater its frequency.

Frequency determines **pitch**— how high or low a sound is.

High-pitched sounds have a higher frequency than low-pitched sounds.

The growl of a lion is a low-pitched sound.

A songbird's call is a high-pitched sound!

ROAR.

chirp.

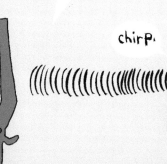

Frequency is measured in **hertz.**

You can measure frequency on an oscilloscope!

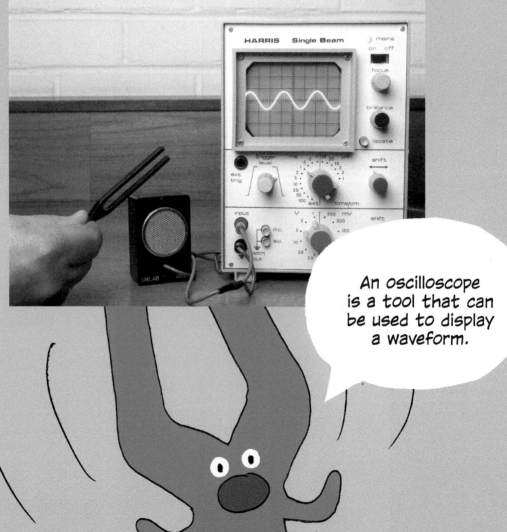

An oscilloscope is a tool that can be used to display a waveform.

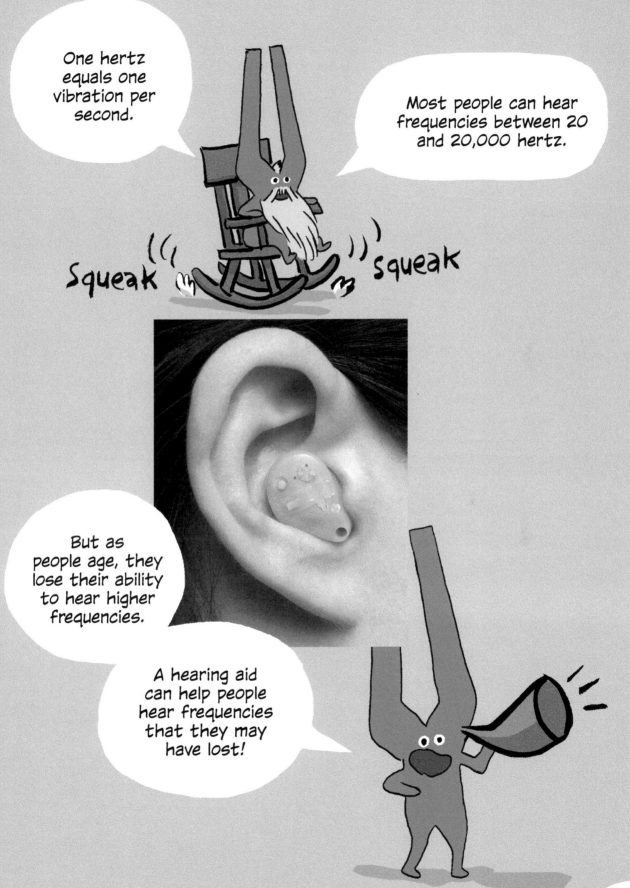

Many kinds of animals can hear sounds with higher or lower frequencies than a human can hear.

Elephants can coordinate their movements through low-frequency sounds and vibrations that are communicated through the ground!

This way, if they become separated, they can find each other.

This whistle makes a high-frequency sound that humans can't hear.

Dogs can, though!

Some animals can hear much softer sounds than people can.

A barn owl can hear the footsteps of its prey.

This allows the owl to hunt in complete darkness.

WHY STUDY SOUND?

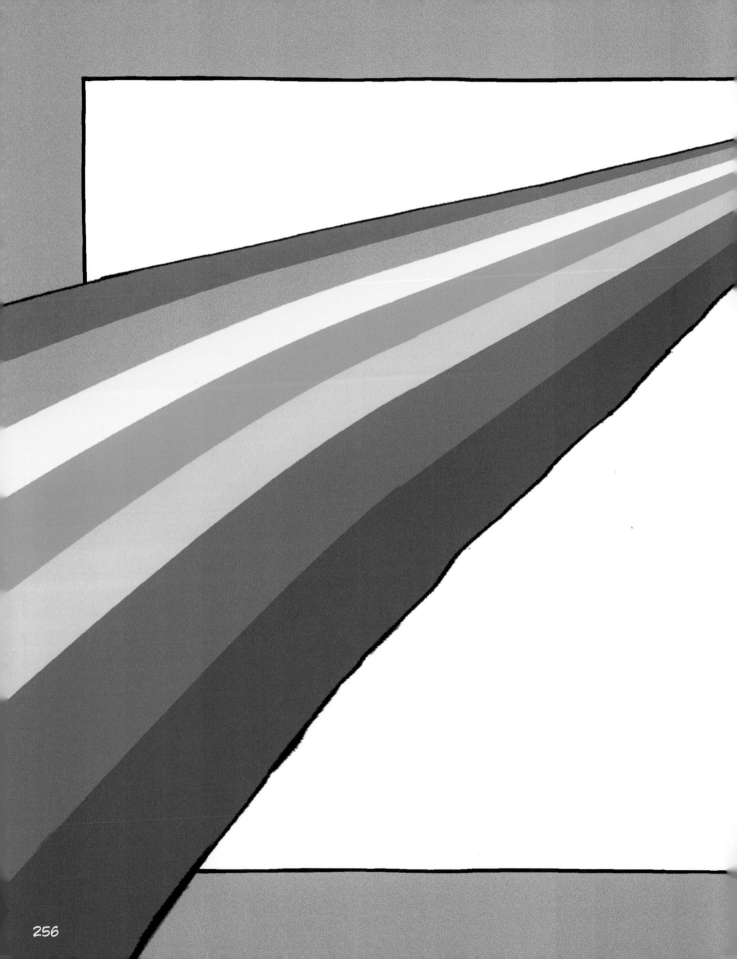

LIGHT

WHAT IS LIGHT?

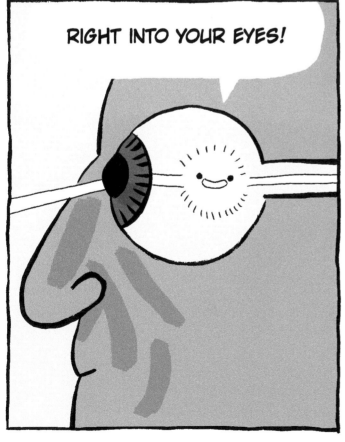

I'm a part of your everyday life.

Let's see how!

Natural light comes from the sun.

It looks white to you.

This is the light that allows you to see.

Without light, you would not have food to eat or air to breathe.

That's because plants and many kinds of ocean life use light from the sun to make food and oxygen.

All the food you eat and the oxygen you breathe can be traced to these living things, and therefore to me!

The energy in fuels also comes from sunlight.

Fossil fuels are made from the remains of living things that died millions of years ago.

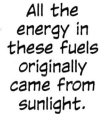

All the energy in these fuels originally came from sunlight.

People use these fuels to produce electric power and to operate machines.

WHAT ARE LIGHT WAVES?

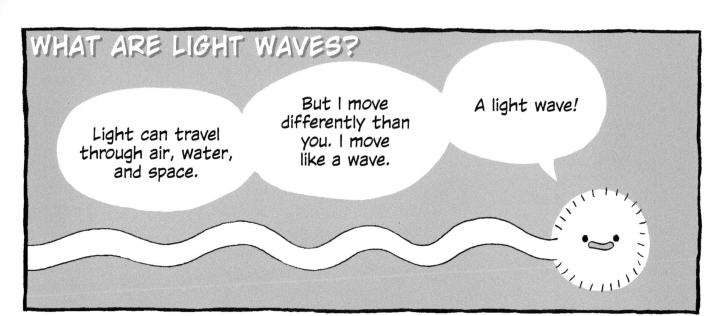

Light can travel through air, water, and space.

But I move differently than you. I move like a wave.

A light wave!

Like ocean waves, light waves are a series of peaks and valleys.

A peak is like the top of the wave.

A valley is the low point.

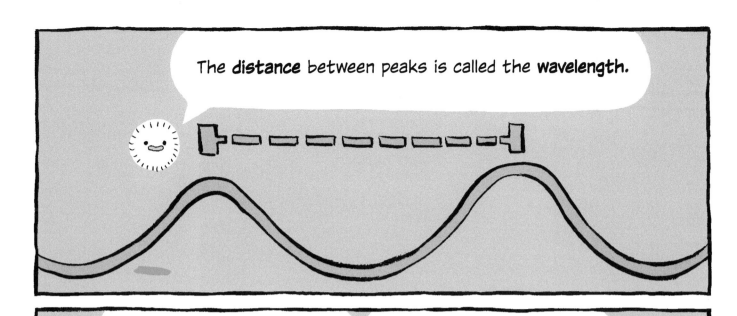

ABSORPTION AND REFLECTION

When light hits an object, several things can happen.

The object can **absorb** me...

...reflect me...

...or let me pass right through it.

Most objects absorb some of the light that hits them.

But they also reflect light.

This reflected light bounces off the object and moves in a different direction.

Some of this reflected light reaches your eyes, allowing you to see.

Objects vary in how much light they absorb or reflect.

Black objects capture most of the light that strikes them.

BLACK

White objects absorb less light and reflect more.

WHITE

That's why it's best to wear a white t-shirt on a hot day!

Shiny surfaces also reflect a lot of light.

Look, I can see myself!

MOVING LIGHT ALONG...

Light can pass through some materials easily and others not at all.

Opaque objects don't let light pass through. They absorb some light and reflect the rest.

This brick wall is opaque. You can't see through it.

Shadows form when an opaque object blocks the path of light.

Transparent objects let most of the light pass through. You can see through them!

This glass window is transparent.

What about a stained-glass window?

It's a **translucent** object.

It lets some light pass through, but only certain colors.

It can also **scatter** the light, making objects on the other side look blurry.

BENDING LIGHT

As you can see, I always find my way around.

But what happens when I pass between air and water?

I move slower through water than through air.

My **speed** changes.

This can cause me to **refract,** or bend.

WHAT ARE COLORS?

White light is made of all the colors of a rainbow.

Red, orange, yellow, green, blue, indigo, and violet...

...ROY G BIV for short!

Each color has a different wavelength.

Light with longer wavelengths is red.

Light with shorter wavelengths is violet.

The other colors have wavelengths between red and violet.

Together, they make up all the colors of a rainbow.

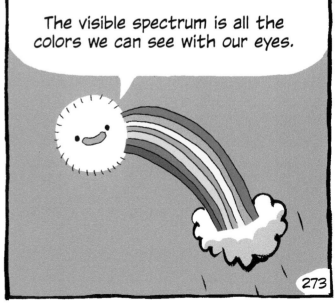

The reflected colors enter your eyes.

For instance, when white light hits this banana...

The banana absorbs all of the colors except yellow.

Only yellow light bounces off the banana.

The yellow light is reflected back into your eyes!

275

HOW DO YOU SEE?

Let's follow the light inside!

Take a look inside the human eye.

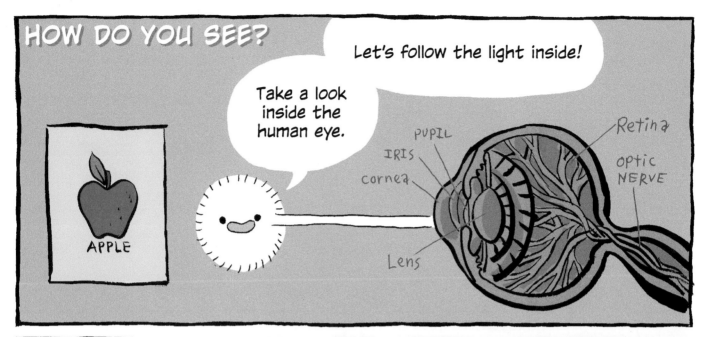

APPLE

PUPIL
IRIS
cornea
Retina
optic NERVE
Lens

The light is refracted slightly as it goes into the outside coat of the eyeball.

The cornea!

Then the light passes through the small opening called the pupil.

The pupil controls how much light enters the eye.

The light then travels through the lens.

The lens refracts the light so that it strikes the retina as a clear image.

The image that the lens focuses onto the retina is upside down.

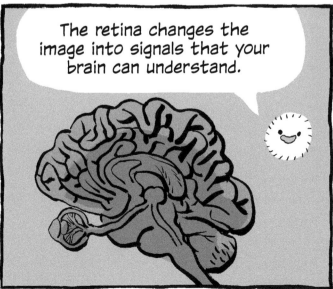

The retina changes the image into signals that your brain can understand.

The brain then uses the signal to make a picture. It also flips the image around.

HOW DO LENSES HELP YOU SEE?

Sometimes people need help to see clearly.

They may wear glasses to help correct their vision.

Glasses are lenses that bend light in a specific way.

Some people are near-sighted. That means they can only see things clearly that are close up.

Others are far-sighted.

They can only see things clearly that are far away.

Lenses are used to correct vision problems.

Near-sighted people need a **concave lens.** A concave lens is thicker at the edges than it is at the center.

This design spreads light waves apart by bending them away from one another.

Objects appear smaller when viewed through the lens.

People who are far-sighted need a **convex lens.**

A convex lens is thicker in the middle than at the edges.

Objects appear larger when viewed through a convex lens.

INVISIBLE LIGHT

Glasses aren't the only way that humans bend light to see.

Another tool that uses lenses is called a telescope.

Telescopes are used to see objects in detail that are extremely far away.

You could use a telescope to magnify an object that is hundreds of thousands of miles away.

Like the moon!

But that only works with the light that you see with your eyes.

Visible light.

The visible light spectrum includes all the colors of the rainbow.

But there are many other forms of light that you can't see!

INFRARED WAVES

Here are a few examples of this "invisible" light.

ULTRAVIOLET WAVES

RADIO WAVES

X RAYS

Bees and other insects use ultraviolet light to see where a flower has nectar!

All of the different kinds of light make up the **electromagnetic spectrum.**

ELECTROMAGNETIC SPECTRUM

WHY STUDY LIGHT?

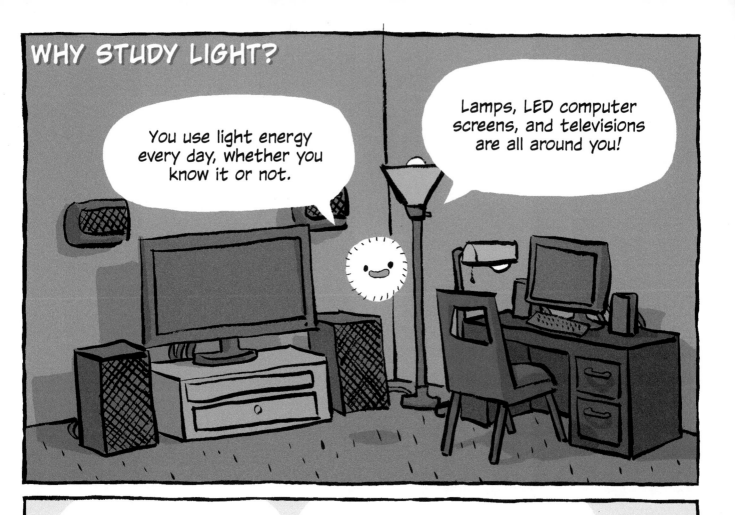

You use light energy every day, whether you know it or not.

Lamps, LED computer screens, and televisions are all around you!

The Internet and other forms of communication are possible because of me!

They use thin underground cables that transmit signals at the speed of light.

That's a fast download!

Right now, scientists are searching the skies with telescopes that can see light that you can't.

One of these instruments, the Hubble Space Telescope, is **orbiting** in space around Earth.

It has produced detailed images captured from the far reaches of the **universe**.

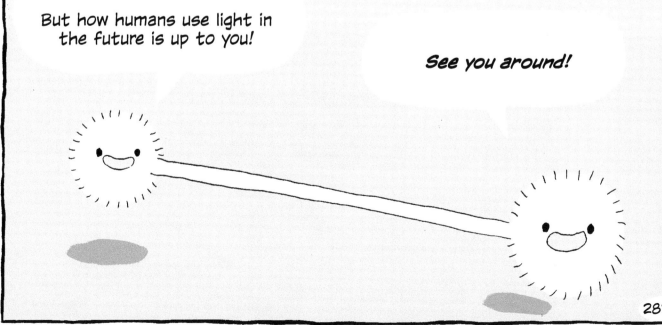

But how humans use light in the future is up to you!

See you around!

WHICH LAW?

Review Newton's Laws of Motion and display the laws where all children can see them. Read the examples below. Ask the group to work together to decide which law of motion is demonstrated by each "scenario."

Law # 1 (inertia):

An object at rest remains at rest or an object in motion continues moving in a straight line at a steady rate until a force acts on it.

Law # 2 (accelerated motion):

The amount of force needed to change the speed of an object depends on the mass of the object and the amount of acceleration or deceleration needed.

Law # 3 (action-reaction pairs):

For every action (force) there is an opposite and equal reaction (force).

1. As an ice skater pushes harder with her muscles, she begins to move faster.

2. A swimmer pushes water backward with his arms, but his body moves forward.

3. A frog leaps off a lily pad. He is pulled downward by gravity and lands on another lily pad instead of continuing the movement in a straight line.

4. A boy paddles the canoe by pulling back on the paddle. The canoe goes forward.

5. It takes more force to get a bike with two people on it moving than a bike with one person.

6. A girl speeds downhill on a sled. The sled hits a rock. The girl is thrown forward and keeps going downhill without the sled.

CATCH A FALLING DOLLAR

Learn a few things about force and motion with this experiment. All you need is a dollar bill and a volunteer from your group to try to catch it. Watch carefully! The bill falls very quickly.

1. The volunteer rests her or his arm on a table with one open hand hanging over the edge of the table.

2. The volunteer should open her or his fingers from the thumb, in a position ready to catch the dollar.

3. Hold the dollar bill between the parted thumb and fingers, with half of the bill above the volunteer's hand.

4. Let the volunteer know that they should try to grab the dollar bill (between fingers and thumb) when it falls.

5. Don't tell the volunteer when you are ready to let the dollar bill go. Just drop it.

6. Let each person in the group try to catch the falling bill.

7. Discuss the results.

THE SOUND OF THE DRUM

When a person hits a drum, a sound is made. The sound travels through the air to his or her ears.

Each drum below has a word about sound.

Each pair of drumsticks below has a description to match one word.

Find the sticks to match each drum. Draw a line to connect them.

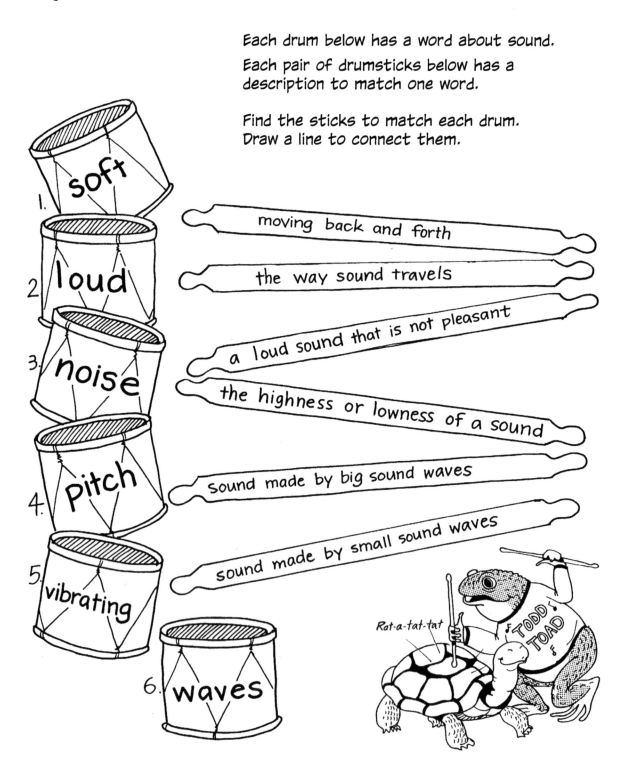

1. soft

2. loud

3. noise

4. pitch

5. vibrating

6. waves

moving back and forth

the way sound travels

a loud sound that is not pleasant

the highness or lowness of a sound

sound made by big sound waves

sound made by small sound waves

Rat-a-tat-tat

TODD TOAD

THE AMAZING, HEARING TEETH

Did you know you can hear through your teeth? Gather a group of friends to try it out! Ask an adult to use metal forks and spoons. Divide the group into pairs, giving each pair a spoon and a fork. Then try this trick to demonstrate how sound travels.

1. Bang the spoon against the fork to make the fork "ring."

2. Hold the fork until the sound begins to fade.

3. When you can't hear the ringing any more, put the handle of the fork between your front teeth.

4. Bite down firmly on the fork handle and listen. Be careful to not bite so hard that you hurt your teeth! After you listen, make sure to clean the fork before your partner takes their turn.

5. Describe and explain what happens.

MAKE A RAINBOW

You can make your own rainbow using a specially shaped piece of solid glass called a prism.

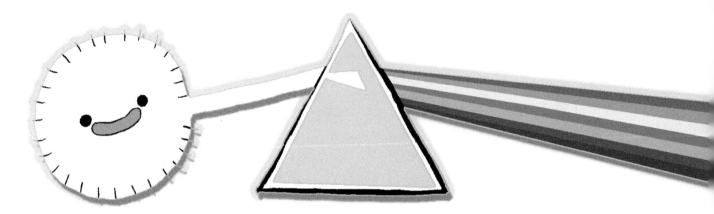

White light shines onto one side of the prism and bends as it travels through the glass. When it comes out at the other side, the light has been refracted and separated into its different colors.

On a sunny day, you can also make a rainbow using a mirror.

YOU WILL NEED:
- water
- modelling clay
- a piece of white card stock or thick paper
- a shallow tray
- a small mirror

1. Fill the tray with water to a depth of about 2.5 centimeters. Place the tray by a window. Draw the curtains so that only a narrow shaft of sunlight enters the room.

2. Rest the mirror in the water at an angle, using modelling clay to make it stand up. Move the tray until the sunlight falls directly on the mirror.

3. Move the card stock around between the tray and the window until you see a rainbow appear on it. You may have to move the mirror to get this just right.

THE CHANGING PENCIL

Use the amazing properties of light for this trick. Watch a pencil grow shorter or longer or fatter—right before your eyes.

1. Place one pencil in the center of the glass of water.

2. Hold the second pencil next to the outside edge of the jar so you can compare it with the pencil inside the jar.

3. Lower your head close to the jar and look straight down at the pencil in the water.

4. Describe what you see.

5. Hold your face close to the side of the jar and look at the pencil inside of it.

6. Describe what you see.

YOU WILL NEED:

- drinking glass, filled with water

- 2 identical pencils, the same length

GOING AROUND IN CIRCLES

Have you ever wondered why planets move in circles around the sun? Find out by setting up this experiment.

YOU WILL NEED:
- a small rubber ball
- a long sock

Without the sun's gravity, Earth would travel through space in a straight line.

WIP
WIP

The sun's gravity pulls Earth toward the sun, but Earth is moving very quickly. It spins around and around the sun.

1. Put the ball into the toe of the sock.

2. Holding the end of the sock, whirl the ball around your head. Do this outside in the open! Make sure no one is nearby!

   Can you feel the ball trying to pull away? To keep it moving in a circle, you have to pull in the other direction.

3. Make sure no one is nearby and whirl the ball around again. What happens when you let go? The ball does not fly off in a circle. It shoots away in a straight line. This is what would happen to a planet or satellite if the force of gravity suddenly disappeared.

   This is how a planet travels around the sun. The planet is trying to escape, and the sun must pull on it to keep it in place. This pull is a gravitational attraction. In the same way, Earth's gravitational attraction is the pull that keeps a satellite circling around it.

DRAW AN ORBIT

Most satellites travel in a specific shape called an ellipse as they orbit the Earth. Try this activity to draw an orbit.

1. Place the sheet of paper on the board and stick in the two push pins about 10 to 12 centimeters apart.

2. Cut a piece of string so that it is about 5 centimeters longer than twice the distance between the push pins. Tie the ends of the string together, and loop it around the pins.

3. Place the pencil within the string as shown. Keeping the string tight, draw a line on the paper. Continue drawing all the way around the pins.

   You will find that you have drawn the shape of an oval. The proper name for it is an ellipse. Most satellites travel around Earth in an orbit that is in the shape of an ellipse.

   Change the size and shape of the ellipse by moving the drawing pins closer together or farther apart.

YOU WILL NEED:
- a sheet of paper
- a wooden board
- a piece of string
- a pencil
- two push pins

MAGNET MAGIC

Have you ever heard of the Indian rope trick? Magicians in India who perform this famous conjuring trick make a rope appear to stand upright from the ground with nothing holding it up.

Other magicians can make objects, and even people, look as if they are floating in the air with nothing holding them up. This is called levitation. We can use magnets to make things levitate, or float in the air. Try it yourself with a simple experiment.

YOU WILL NEED:
- cotton thread
- a paper clip
- sticky tape
- a sheet of paper
- a strong magnet

1. Tie one end of the cotton thread to a paper clip.

2. Tape the other end of the thread to the top of a table, using sticky tape.

3. Can you make the thread stand up without letting the magnet touch the paper clip?

4. Pass a sheet of paper between the magnet and the paper clip to show that they are not touching.

MAPPING A MAGNETIC FIELD

Although you can't see magnetism, you can make
a map of a magnetic field that will help you to see
where and how magnetism works.

1. Place the magnet in the middle of a large
   piece of paper and draw around it in pencil to
   mark its position.

2. Put the compass near the magnet. Draw a
   short arrow from the compass to the magnet,
   showing the direction the needle is pointing.

3. Move the compass to another position. Draw
   another arrow showing the direction of the
   needle. Move the compass to about 20 places
   around the magnet. Draw short arrows in
   each location.

4. The arrows on your map form curved lines that
   run from the north pole of the magnet to the
   south pole. The lines are drawn closer to
   each other near the poles, where
   the magnetism is strongest.
   Away from the poles,
   where the magnetism
   is weaker, the lines
   are drawn farther
   apart from each
   other.

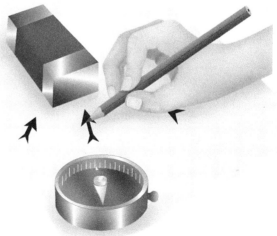

WARMING AIR AND WATER

Why does hot air take up more space than cold air? Air is a mixture of gases. Heating the air puts more energy into these gases. The tiny particles of gas rush about faster and faster and hit each other more often. The particles bounce off each other and push out to take up more space. So the gas expands.

You can try this experiment to show what happens when you warm air and water.

YOU WILL NEED:
- modelling clay
- a drinking straw
- a glass bottle
- a bowl of water
- a cloth

1. Using modelling clay, seal a drinking straw into the neck of a glass bottle. Hold the bottle upside down and dip the end of the straw into a bowl of water.

2. Now wrap a warm, wet cloth around the bottle to heat the air inside. What is escaping from the end of the straw? Explain why.

3. Now replace the warm, wet cloth with a cold one. What happens to the air inside the bottle? Describe what you see. Explain.

4. This time, fill the bottle with cold water before you fit the straw. Some of the water should rise a little way up the straw. Now stand the bottle in a bowl of hot water to heat the water inside the bottle. What happens? Explain.

The particles in a liquid are not rushing about as fast as the particles in a gas. They slide past each other and hit each other less often than the particles in a gas. But warming a liquid makes the particles move faster, making the liquid expand.

Be careful with hot water.

JUMPING AND MELTING

When a solid melts, its molecules break free of each other and start moving about as a liquid. As a liquid gets hotter, its molecules move faster and faster until they break free of the liquid surface and become a gas.

Make this model to show how molecules jump around more as a substance gets hotter.

YOU WILL NEED:

- empty glass water bottle
- very cold water
- coin large enough to cover the opening of the bottle completely

1. Rinse the empty bottle with very cold water or leave the bottle in the refrigerator for at least 10 minutes.

2. Spread some water over the lip of the bottle opening with your finger.

3. Place the coin over the wet lip of the bottle opening. After about three minutes, as the air in the bottle warms and expands, the coin will click up and down. Try putting the bottle and coin in a sunny window. What happens?

4. Describe what you see.

IS IT A CONDUCTOR?

How can you tell which materials are conductors and which are insulators? Find out by setting up a special experiment.

1. Tape the bare end of a piece of wire to the top of the battery.

2. Using the screwdriver, connect the other end of the wire to one of the screws on the bulb holder.

3. Tape one end of the second piece of wire to the bottom of the battery. Do not connect the other end.

4. Connect one end of the third piece of wire to the other side of the bulb holder. Do not connect the other end.

5. To make sure your equipment works, hold the insulated parts of the two free wires and touch together the two bare ends of wire. The bulb should light up. If you separate the two ends, the bulb should go out. Do not touch any bare electric wires.

YOU WILL NEED:

- three pieces of plastic-coated wire, 20 centimeters long, with bare ends

- a screwdriver

- masking tape

- a 1.5-volt battery

- a 1.5-volt penlight bulb and miniature bulb holder

- a collection of objects, such as a toothbrush, pen, ruler, nail, fork, pencil case, eraser, and coin

Adult supervision required!

6. Now find out which objects are conductors. Place one bare wire at one end of an object and the second bare wire at the other end. If the bulb lights up, is the object a conductor or an insulator? Do the same with each object.

7. Now write down the names of all those objects that you found to be good conductors. Can you find something that they all have in common? Are all the conductors made from the same type of material?

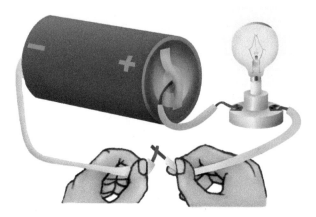

MAKING A SWITCH

A switch is a way of turning an electric current on and off. When a switch is turned off, the electric circuit is broken. No electric current can flow around the circuit. When a switch is turned on, the circuit is complete and the current can flow.

You can make a simple switch to use in your experiments.

1. Attach a piece of wire to each push pin. Push one pin into one of the flat sides of the wood. Push the second pin through the end loop of the paper clip and into the wood. The push pins should be about 1 centimeter apart.

   Make sure the clip is held in place by one push pin but can still turn around and touch the other pin. This is the switch.

Adult supervision required!

YOU WILL NEED:

- a small block of soft wood, about 8 cm x 4 cm x 1 cm
- three pieces of plastic-coated wire, each about 25 cm long, with bare ends
- bulb holder
- a 6-volt light bulb
- a 6-volt battery
- a screwdriver
- paper clip
- two metal push pins or thumb tacks

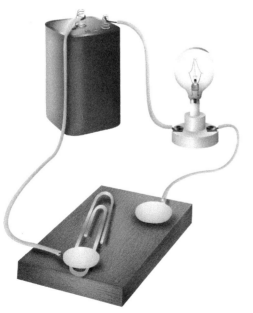

2. To test the switch, connect the free end of one of the wires to one of the battery terminals. Connect the third wire to the other battery terminal and to the bulb holder.

   Connect the free wire on the switch to the free screw on the bulb holder.

   Turn the paper clip around so that it is touching both push pins. What happens? Now turn the paper clip away from the free pin. What happens?

MAKE A SPOOL TRACTOR

Find out how a thread spool tractor uses a twisted rubber band to store potential energy.

1. Thread the rubber band through the center of the spool. Cut one of the toothpicks so that it is shorter than the diameter of the spool and push it through the loop of the band at one end of the spool. Pull the rubber band at the other end of the spool tight to hold the short toothpick in place.

2. Thread the free end of the rubber band through the hole in the candle. Insert the second toothpick through the rubber band loop and turn the toothpick tightly to wind up the tractor.

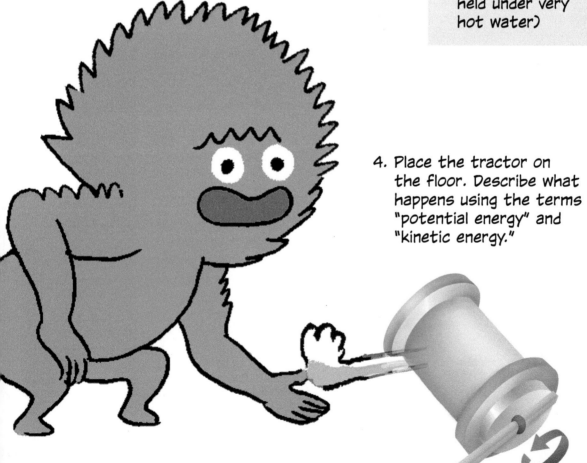

YOU WILL NEED:

- a thread spool
- a rubber band
- two toothpicks
- scissors
- a 1.25-centimeter circular slice of a candle with a hole in the center (to slice the candle, use a dinner knife that has been held under very hot water)

Adult supervision required!

4. Place the tractor on the floor. Describe what happens using the terms "potential energy" and "kinetic energy."

MAKE YOUR OWN TURBINE

Follow the directions to make a simple impulse water turbine.

YOU WILL NEED:
- a modelling knife
- heavy card stock
- scissors
- a cork
- a metal knitting needle

1. Push the knitting needle carefully through the center of the cork.

Adult supervision required!

2. Ask an adult to help you cut six slots round the edge of the cork. Make sure the slots are not cut right to the center of the cork.

3. Cut six paddle shapes out of the card stock and slide one into each slot. Old photographs will also make good paddles. (Make sure you get permission before cutting up a photograph.) This is your paddle-wheel.

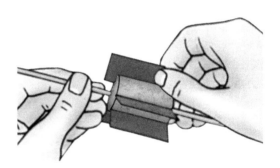

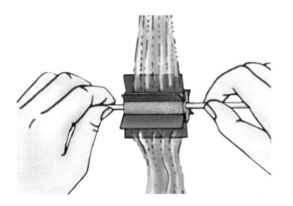

4. Loosely hold each end of the needle and place your paddle-wheel under a tap of cold running water. It will spin freely between your fingers.

5. Describe what you see.

WHAT KIND OF CHANGE?

In each of the events below a change in matter is taking place. Is it a physical change or a chemical change? Next to each event, place the label P for physical change or C for chemical change.

_____ 1. spoiling food

_____ 2. a glass breaking

_____ 3. freezing popsicles

_____ 4. making salt water to gargle

_____ 5. burning leaves

_____ 6. a rusting bicycle

_____ 7. fireworks exploding

_____ 8. frying an egg

_____ 9. evaporating water

_____ 10. melting butter

_____ 11. glassblower blowing glass

_____ 12. whipping cream

_____ 13. bleaching hair

_____ 14. burning toast

_____ 15. squeezing lemons to make lemonade

_____ 16. hammering wood to make a birdhouse

CLEAN YOUR PENNIES

Use this solution to make old pennies look like new.

YOU WILL NEED:
- a glass jar
- measuring spoons
- water
- vinegar
- salt
- paper towels
- dirty pennies

Do not drink the solution!

1. Mix 3 tablespoons of vinegar and 1 tablespoon of salt in the jar.

2. Drop the dirty pennies in the jar.

3. Wait a few minutes.

4. Remove the pennies, rinse them with water, and dry them with paper towels.

5. Why did the pennies become clean when they were dropped into the solution? Do some research to find out!

A solution is a homogeneous mixture in which one substance (a solute) is dissolved in another (a solvent).

TEN WORDS OR LESS

Matter is the material that makes up all things in the universe. Each substance has properties. In ten words or less, write a definition or explanation of each word below.

1. weight

2. density

3. freezing point

4. boiling point

5. magnetism

6. mass

7. volume

8. viscosity

9. physical property

10. chemical property

COMMON COMBINATIONS

A compound is a combination of one or more elements. The elements have been chemically combined—meaning that the nature of each individual substance is changed to produce a new substance.

Read the names of the everyday compounds below. Use science references to research and find the chemical formula for as many of these compounds as possible.

1. marble

2. bleach

3. table salt

4. baking soda

5. sand

6. hydrogen peroxide

7. lime

8. milk of magnesia

9. sugar

10. candle wax

11. Freon

12. ammonia

ANSWER KEY

page 286

1. # 2	4. # 3
2. # 3	5. # 2
3. # 1	6. # 1

page 287

What Happened?
The force (gravity) causes objects to move faster as they fall. The dollar bill falls so fast that the brain can't receive the message and send it back to the fingers fast enough for the person to grab it.

page 288

1. sound made by small sound waves
2. sound made by big sound waves
3. a loud sound that is not pleasant
4. the highness or lowness of a sound
5. moving back and forth
6. the way sound travels

page 289

What Happened?
Solids such as your teeth and the bones in your ears are better conductors of sound than air is. Sound is caused by the vibrations of the fork. Placing the fork against your teeth allows the teeth to carry the vibrations through your head to the bones in your ears. You will be able to hear the ringing inside your head.

page 290

What Happened?
White light shines onto one side of the prism and bends as it travels through the glass. When it comes out at the other side, the light has been refracted and separated into its different colors.

page 291

What Happened?
When light travels between two substances, its rays become bent. The light traveling from the air to the glass and the water bend. This bending light causes an object to look smaller or larger, depending on the angle of viewing.

page 292

What Happened?
When the ball is whirled, the ball does not fly off in a circle. It shoots away in a straight line. This is what would happen to a planet or satellite if the force of gravity suddenly disappeared. This is how a planet travels around the sun. The sun's gravity pulls the planet toward the sun, but it is moving very quickly. It spins around and around the sun.

page 293

What Happened?
The drawing is in the shape of an oval, or ellipse. Most satellites travel around Earth in an orbit that is an ellipse.

page 294

What Happened?
The magnet made the paper clip levitate, or float, in the air. Levitation happens when objects appear to be floating in the air with nothing holding them up, when the magnet is actually pulling the object in one direction.

page 295

What Happened?
The map of a magnetic field helps to show where and how magnetism works.

page 296

What Happened?
When air is heated, it expands to take up more space. Heating air puts more energy into the

gases, making particles move faster, bounce off each other, and take up more space. When a gas cools, it contracts to take up less space. The particles in a liquid are not rushing about as fast as the particles in a gas. They slide past each other and hit each other less often than the particles in a gas. But warming a liquid makes the particles move faster, making the liquid expand.

page 297

What Happened?
As the air in the bottle warms and expands, the coin will click up and down. When placed in a sunny window, the coin will click faster.

page 298

What Happened?
If the bulb lights up, the object is a conductor. If the bulb does not light up, the object is an insulator.

page 299

What Happened?
When the paper clip touches both drawing pins, the light turns on. When the paper clip is away from the drawing pin, the light turns off.

page 300

What Happened?
The thread spool tractor uses a twisted rubber band to store potential energy. When the tractor is let go on the floor, the potential energy of the tractor turns into kinetic energy and the tractor moves.

page 301

What Happened?
The paddle wheel spins freely because the wheel turned the potential energy of water into kinetic energy. When the water flows onto the paddles, it forces the wheel to spin.

page 302

1. C
2. P
3. P
4. P
5. C
6. C
7. C
8. C
9. P
10. P
11. P
12. P
13. C
14. C
15. P
16. P

page 303

How It Works:
The vinegar (acetic acid) combined with the salt (sodium chloride) to make a new substance called hydrochloric acid. The hydrochloric acid is able to clean the pennies.

page 304

Answers will vary.
Possible answers:
1. force of gravity pulling on an object
2. amount of mass in a particular unit of mass (OR, mass of the material divided by its volume)
3. temperature at which the liquid form becomes solid
4. temperature at which the liquid form turns to gas
5. property of attracting certain other substances
6. amount of matter in an object
7. amount of space taken up by an object
8. describes how a substance pours
9. characteristic that can be observed
10. characteristics that describes how one substance will react with another

page 305

1. $CaCO_3$
2. $NaClO$
3. NaC_l
4. CH_4
5. SiO_2
6. $H2O_2$
7. CaO
8. $Mg(OH)_2$
9. $C_{12}H_{22}O_{11}$
10. CH_2
11. CF_2C_{l2}
12. NH_3

GLOSSARY

A

absorb to take in and hold rather than reflect.

acceleration a change in the speed or direction of an object.

acid rain rain that has become acidic. It is caused by pollution in the air.

amplitude the amount of energy in a wave.

atmosphere the mixture of gases in contact with Earth's surface and extending far above.

atom one of the basic units of matter.

attract to pull one object toward another.

B

biofuel any energy-producing substance made from living things.

black hole a region of space whose gravitational force is so strong that nothing can escape it.

C

chemical change a change in which one substance is converted into one or more substances with different properties.

chemical energy energy that is stored inside the molecules of a chemical.

circuit a path for electric current. A circuit is usually made of metal wire.

cochlea a spiral-shaped cavity of the inner ear.

compound a substance that contains more than one kind of atom.

concave lens a lens that is thicker at the edges than in the center. Objects appear smaller when viewed through a concave lens.

condensation the changing of a gas or a vapor into a liquid.

condense to make denser or more compact.

conduction the movement of heat through a material.

conductor something that allows heat, electricity, light, sound, or another form of energy to pass through it.

contract to decrease in size.

convection the transfer of heat by the movement of gas or liquid.

convex lens a lens that is thicker in the center than at the edges. Objects appear larger when viewed through a convex lens.

crest the highest point of a sound wave. The crest represents the area where particles in the wave are crowded together.

D

density the amount of matter in a particular volume of a substance.

distance the amount of space between two points.

E

eardrum the part of the ear that vibrates in response to sounds.

echo a reflected sound.

echolocation the use of sound by certain animals to sense their surroundings. Bats and dolphins use echolocation.

electric charge a build-up of electricity.

electric current a steady flow of electrons through a material, most commonly a metal.

electric generator a machine that produces electric power from mechanical energy (motion).

electric motor a machine that produces mechanical energy (motion) from electric power.

electromagnet a temporary magnet produced by the flow of an electric current.

electromagnetic spectrum the entire range of electromagnetic energy, including visible light and forms of light that cannot be seen by the human eye. Electromagnetic energy is made up of electric and magnetic waves.

electromagnetism the relationship between electricity and magnetism.

electron a kind of particle that circles around the nucleus of an atom. Electrons have a negative electric charge.

element a substance made of only one kind of atom.

engineer a person who plans and builds engines, machines, roads, bridges, canals, forts, or the like.

evaporate to change from a liquid into a gas.

expand to increase in size.

F

force a push or a pull.

fossil fuel a fuel formed from the long-dead remains of living things. Fossil fuels include coal, natural gas, and petroleum (oil).

frequency the number of sound waves or light waves that pass by one point in a given time.

friction rubbing between objects that slows them down and produces heat.

G

gravity a force that attracts all objects toward one another.

H

hertz a unit used to measure sound frequency. One hertz equals one cycle (sound wave) per second.

I

inclined plane a simple machine shaped like a ramp.

inertia the tendency of objects to stay at rest or stay in motion.

insulator something that prevents the passage of electricity, heat, or sound.

K

kinetic energy the energy of motion.

L

lever a simple machine consisting of a rod or bar that rests and turns on a support called a fulcrum.

lubrication the act of making machinery smooth and easy to work by putting on oil or grease.

M

magnetic field an area of force around a magnet.

magnetism a force produced by the motion of electrons in a material.

mass the amount of matter in an object.

matter what all things are made of.

mechanical force the force applied when two objects touch each other.

metal any of a large group of elements that includes copper, gold, iron, lead, silver, tin, and other elements that share similar qualities.

microbe a living organism of very small size.

molecule two or more atoms chemically bonded together.

motion a change in position.

N

neutron a kind of particle inside the nucleus of an atom. Neutrons have no electric charge.

nonmetal materials that do not have the properties of metals. Wood, glass, plastic, and rock are examples of nonmetals.

nonrenewable resource a resource that cannot be replenished once it is used. Fossil fuels are nonrenewable resources.

nucleus the center of an atom. Protons and neutrons are inside the nucleus.

nutrient a nourishing substance, especially as an element or ingredient of food.

O

opaque describes an object that does not allow light to pass through it.

orbit (n.) the path of one object around another determined by gravity. For example, the path of Earth around the sun is an orbit; (v.) to revolve around an object.

P

periodic table a chart that lists the known chemical elements arranged according to their characteristics.

physical change a change in which matter changes shape or form.

physics the science that deals with matter and energy.

pitch the highness or lowness of a sound.

pole one of two poles of a magnet. Magnetic fields are strongest near magnetic poles.

pollution waste and harmful substances produced by human activity and released into the environment.

potential energy energy stored in an object or system that can be converted into kinetic energy.

prism a special piece of glass or plastic that can refract (bend) light to produce a spectrum of colors.

property a quality or characteristic of something. Properties of matter can be used to describe objects.

proton a kind of particle inside the nucleus of an atom. Protons have a positive electric charge.

pulley a simple machine made of a rope or chain wrapped around a spinning wheel.

R

radiation energy given off as waves or small bits of matter. Heat from the sun is one example of radiation.

reflect to throw back light, heat, sound, or other form of energy. Reflection occurs when energy or an object bounces off a surface.

refract what occurs when light bends as it passes from one substance to another.

renewable resource natural resources, such as trees, that can be replaced after they have been used.

repel to force apart or away.

repulsion the action of repelling or condition of being repelled.

S

scatter to separate and drive off in different directions.

screw a simple machine shaped like a ramp wrapped around a central shaft.

simple machine any of six basic tools that change the way force is used to do work.

smog a form of air pollution that resembles a combination of smoke and fog in the air.

solar of the sun.

solar system the sun and all the planets, satellites, comets, and other heavenly bodies that revolve around it.

solution a mixture in which one substance is dissolved (mixed completely) in another.

sound wave energy that moves through a material, such as air or water, as a vibration.

speed the distance traveled in a certain time.

states of matter the different forms of matter. The most familiar are solid, liquid, and gas.

static electricity the build-up of electrons on the surface of an object.

suspension a heterogeneous (uneven) mixture of a liquid and a solid in which the solid settles to the bottom if left undisturbed.

switch a device that opens or closes a gap in a circuit.

T

thermal energy the force that makes particles of matter vibrate and move.

thermometer a tool for measuring temperature.

translucent describes an object that allows only some light to pass through it.

transparent describes an object that allows nearly all light to pass through it.

trough the lowest point of a sound wave. The trough represents the area where particles in the wave are spread farthest apart.

turbine an engine or motor in which a wheel is made to revolve by the force of water, steam, hot gases, or air. Turbines are often used to turn generators that produce electric power.

U

ultrasound sound that is too high-pitched for human beings to hear.

universe everything that exists everywhere, including Earth, the stars, planets, and other heavenly bodies.

V

visible spectrum the band of colors that make up white light.

volume the amount of space something takes up.

W

water vapor water in the state of a gas.

wavelength the distance between peaks of a wave.

wedge a simple machine shaped like two inclined planes placed back to back with an edge that cuts or slices.

wheel and axle a simple machine with a big wheel attached to a post.

INDEX

E

F

X

ACKNOWLEDGMENTS

14-15   © Alchemy/Alamy Images;
         © Shutterstock

26-27   © Shutterstock;
         © Peter Dean, Shutterstock

28-29   © Oleksandr Kostiuchenko,
         Shutterstock; © Shutterstock

38-39   © Stanislav Komogorov,
         Shutterstock; NASA

54-55   © Christina Richards,
         Shutterstock; © Shutterstock

56-57   © David Kocherhans,
         Shutterstock ; © Shutterstock

68-69   © Oleg Fedorenko, Dreamstime;
         © Farzin Salimi, Dreamstime;
         © Steven Newton, Shutterstock

70-71   © Bill Mack, Shutterstock;
         © Robert Fullerton, Shutterstock

74-75   © Shutterstock; © Cathy
         Keifer, Shutterstock;
         © Glenn Young, Shutterstock

80-81   © Brian A. Jackson, Shutterstock;
         © Shutterstock; © Pierre-Jean
         Durieu, Shutterstock

94-95   © Michaela Stejskalova,
         Shutterstock; © Andy Crawford,
         Dorling Kindersley/Getty Images

104-105 WORLD BOOK illustration by Paul
         Perreault and Brenda Tropinski;
         © Dreamstime

122-123 © Tianyu Han, Shutterstock ;
         © Filipe Frazao, Shutterstock;
         © Alinute Silzeviciute,
         Shutterstock; WORLD BOOK
         illustration

128-129 © Dreamstime; © Shutterstock

138-139 © Dreamstime; © Dreamstime;
         © Shutterstock

150-151 © Les Cunliffe, Dreamstime;
         © Mark Cinotti, Shutterstock;
         © Shutterstock; © Shutterstock

152-153 © Shutterstock; © Michael
         Chamberlin, Shutterstock;
         © FoodCollection/SuperStock;
         © iStock

166-167 WORLD BOOK illustration by
         Linda Kinnaman

186-187 © Yury Kosourov, Shutterstock;
         © Shutterstock

190-191 © Brittany Courville,
         Shutterstock; © Shutterstock

192-193 © June M. Sobrito, Dreamstime;
         © Dreamstime

204-205 © Sebastian Kaulitzki,
         Shutterstock; © Shutterstock

206-207 WORLD BOOK diagram by Paul
         Perreault; © Shutterstock

216-217 © Ivan Smuk, Shutterstock;
         © Evgeny Tomeev, Shutterstock

236-237 © sciencephotos/Alamy Images;
         © Igor Chekalin, Shutterstock

242-243 © Taxi/Getty Images;
         © Shutterstock;
         © Shutterstock

250-251 © sciencephotos/Alamy Images;
         © David Gunn, iStock

260-261 © Shutterstock; © RIA Novosti/
         Alamy Images

266-267 © Shutterstock; © Alexander
         Mak, Shutterstock; © FORGET
         Patrick/SAGAPHOTO/Alamy
         Images

270-271 © Shutterstock; © Igor
         Plotnikov, Shutterstock